Revision Lessons
You'll Love to Teach

Highly Motivating Lessons That Give Students Tools, Skills, and Strategies
to Make Meaningful Revisions—and Empower Them as Writers

**Ruth Townsend Story
and Cathleen F. Greenwood**

■ SCHOLASTIC

New York • Toronto • London • Auckland • Sydney
Mexico City • New Delhi • Hong Kong • Buenos Aires

To the students and teachers who come to our classes and workshops, who consistently provide us with inspiration, motivation, and laughter—and to our husbands, daughters, and sons, who continue to tell us to go for it.

ACKNOWLEDGMENTS

Our approach to the teaching and learning of writing is made possible by the many fine teachers, writers, and researchers whose work has informed and motivated us to make the teaching and learning of writing relevant and rewarding.

We are especially indebted …

to Nancie Atwell and Linda Rief for showing us why and how to put student workshop pedagogy at the heart of the reading and writing classroom.

to Janet Angelillo, Randy Bomer, Peter Elbow, Ralph Fletcher, Joanne Portalupi, Georgia Heard, Donald Murray, Tom Romano, and William Zinsser for their research and writing on how to make writing come alive.

to Donald Graves for all he does to support teachers and students, and especially for his book *Testing Is Not Teaching* (Heinemann, 2002).

to Rippowam Cisqua School in Bedford, New York, especially Cathy Greenwood's students, who write and revise like crazy every year, and boldly submit their writing to the world; and to Bob Whelan, Susie Danziger, and Aggy Duveen in the Development Office with Tim Coffey, photographer, for providing the wonderful photos that accompany our text.

to Scholastic, especially David Goddy, Vice President, Terry Cooper, Vice President/Publisher, Eileen Hillebrand, Vice President, Susan Kolwicz, Senior Marketing Manager, and Virginia Dooley, Editorial Director, for their belief and support of our work; and especially to Merryl Maleska Wilbur, Development and Project Editor, and Joanna Davis-Swing, Executive Editor, who worked tirelessly to shape and hone this book. Without the support and encouragement of these fine people, this book could not have been written.

We also thank the following people who read and responded to this book in helpful and positive ways: Kylene Beers, NCTE President; Carol Jago, NCTE Vice President; Kim Ford, teacher at Cyprus Junior High School, Tennessee, and Department Editor, *Voices from the Middle* (NCTE); and Linda Rief, teacher at Oyster River Middle School, Durham, New Hampshire.

Cover design: Jaime A. Lucero
Cover photos, top row, l to r: © American Images Inc/Digital Vision/Getty Images; © Ryan McVay/Photodisc/Getty Images; © Inti St Clair/Digital Vision/Getty Images; bottom row, l to r: © Ryan McVay/Photodisc/Getty Images; © Ableimages/Digital Vision/Getty Images
Interior design: LDL Designs
Interior photos courtesy of the authors

ISBN-13: 978-0-439-93445-9
ISBN-10: 0-439-93445-1
Copyright © 2008 by Ruth Townsend Story and Cathleen F. Greenwood.
All rights reserved. Published by Scholastic Inc.
Printed in the U.S.A.
1 2 3 4 5 6 7 8 9 10   40   14 13 12 11 10 09 08

Table of Contents

INTRODUCTION:
Motivating Revision Through Real Writing

t is a bright and sunny morning. You spent a dark and stormy weekend grading the compositions for your class, underlining strong sentences and putting wavy lines under parts that needed tightening. You have marked spelling and punctuation errors and included symbols such as *AWK* and *RELEVANCE*? and *R/O* in the margins. Now you write on the board the aim of today's lesson:

Review common errors in your compositions and revise for more powerful writing.

A hand shoots up:

"Are we getting our papers back today?"

"Yes," you answer, "but first we are going over some of the mistakes many of you made."

Ignoring soft groans of disappointment and resignation, you present your carefully planned lesson on the most common errors, including underlining the title of a book, avoiding run-ons, and punctuating dialogue. You even include student samples, carefully retyped and slightly altered, of course, to avoid identifying the writers. You really worked hard all weekend to prepare for this lesson.

Now you ask if there are any questions and remind students that you are here on Wednesday for extra help and writing conferences.

All eyes are on the folder on your desk; it is throbbing with graded writing that is yearning to be returned to its owners, the red ink practically glowing through the folder's manila cover. You distribute the papers, face-down on the desks, to their owners. Eager eyes scan for grades and comments, and then papers are tucked into binders and book bags.

Another hand goes up. "Oh, good," you chirp. "What's your question?"

"Um, what was the class average?"

Alas, no one asks about your carefully phrased comments and suggestions for revision. No one questions your editorial symbols or the reasons for the corrections you made of errors in spelling and grammar. No one asks to hear the best pieces read aloud. No one requests a writing conference. No one even

offers to revise for extra credit, even though that involves simply making the corrections you have written on the papers. You try another tack: "You can improve your grades if you revise your compositions." No takers. Over and out.

The writing is done as far as your students are concerned. You know they have just begun the writing process, that they have written nothing more than first drafts, that they have clearly neither crafted nor revised or edited their compositions beyond running spell-check. Your students have not critically reexamined their work as to clarity of purpose, selection of relevant details, logic of organization, or appropriateness of word choice and sentence structure. There is little chance these compositions will ever be revisited or revised because the students have moved on and so must you.

So what to do about this? You could bemoan this generation and its need for instant gratification. Criticize parents and government mandates that emphasize grades and standardized testing. Rant about how the media and its sound bites and megabytes have limited deep thinking, the critical element of clear writing. And be sure to blame the time-sucking black holes of the Internet and instant messaging that are wearing out the thumbs and attention spans of anyone under 50.

Teaching English in the 21st Century

Once you have done all your moaning and groaning, try this: Get over it and get real. This is actually an amazing time to be an English teacher. This generation is into communication in a big way. So take heart; they want to write and they want to tell stories. In fact, many of them do it for hours on end, every day, through e-mails, instant messaging, blogs, text messaging on cell phones, and songs.

Some things haven't changed, and young people still love to connect with one another and the rest of the world. They really do want to be heard. They also want to be sure they are communicating their messages and stories clearly so that others will understand them and respond. After all, they're only human.

Right, you say, but how do we get our students to write and revise their writing so they achieve these goals and improve their writing? The key is to have them *write for real reasons and real audiences*. Brace yourself: This means more than writing for a good grade (the reason), or for the teacher or SAT scoring panel (the audience). These are certainly valid reasons and audiences, but they do not make a writer's heart sing, and they are only a few of the many reasons and audiences that compel teens to write—and therefore make them want to revise.

At the heart of inspiring and empowering students to revise their writing, then, is generating student writing that involves choice in topics and genres, time for development, response from fellow writers, and real purposes and audiences for their writing. After all, aren't all of these conditions present in their writing of choice: blogs, e-mail, and instant messaging?

A Paradigm Shift

Instituting writing for real might involve a paradigm shift in your assignments and lessons, but once you decide, it's really not that difficult. You will present options for expository essays and book or movie reviews that have the potential to be published in school and local papers, (safe) Web sites for teen writers, and magazines that publish young writers. You will discover that many of these publications/audiences are also eager to publish your students' fiction, memoirs, poetry, and even their essays. You will begin to notice the writing contests that fill your mailbox, and you'll share them with students. You will require each student to submit at least one writing piece each term to a publication or contest. It's all for real audiences and real reasons—and something exciting will happen in your classroom.

Once your students realize their writing is going beyond the teacher's desk, the motivation to revise becomes as real as their writing. You'll hear such comments as "Oh, you mean I can send this letter to the author? In that case, I want to fix some things." And "I wonder if he (or she) will write back. I'd really like that."

And be sure to pass out chocolate kisses or some small treat for the class when the first student piece gets a response or gets published or earns honorable mention in a contest. You probably want to stock up on those goodies for celebrating published or winning writers. You might even be faced with the best situation a teacher can imagine: students who will be motivated to revise their writing so that people will really want to read, publish, and reward their efforts. (See page 14 for a list of recommended opportunities for students to publish their own writing for real audiences.)

PART I
Our Approach: Student Ownership of Writing and Revising

Our approach to teaching writing is based on our core belief that students must take ownership of their writing and revising. To help students take that step, teachers must provide real writing opportunities that engage them, and in Part I we discuss how to design relevant lessons and assignments.

Then in Part II, we introduce our system for giving students ownership of writing and revision strategies they can use to strengthen their writing. You'll find, as we have year after year, that students are eager to work on their writing when it's done for real purposes *and* they have the tools they need to do so effectively. Our system consists of a list of revision techniques, which we call the Decoder List of Revision Strategies. This list is essentially a collection of brief definitions that will remind students of revision strategies they've learned and can apply in their own work. But that's not all. We pair the Decoder List with a Personal Record of Strategies and Skills, which students create from the feedback we give on their work. Students copy a shorthand notation that we write in response to a piece, and then they look up the definition of the strategy on the Decoder List and write it on their own record. On their next writing assignment, they consult their Personal Record and apply the strategies they've recorded. It's a simple way to empower students with the tools they need to become successful writers. When introducing the system, we encourage you to discuss the essentials of real writing and use the language of revision so that you and your students are literally speaking the same language from the get-go.

In Part III, we provide lessons that show students how writing works and teach students how to revise to include

those qualities in their own writing. The lessons are organized into five units. Each unit kicks off with a focused revision exercise, which teaches a specific strategy and offers an immediate opportunity to try it out. These exercises can also be used as writing "workouts" to give students plenty of practice.

Following the revision exercise is a series of lessons that gives students opportunities to write for real audiences. Each unit offers students choice in topic, models of the genre to study, time for writing and revising, and feedback from other writers—all elements that foster student ownership. After students have ample opportunity to revise a piece, they submit it to you for what we call a Teacher Edit. At this stage you offer editorial comments, refer students to revision strategies on the Decoder List, and give grades if you wish.

Each lesson and revision exercise is linked to the Decoder List of Revision Strategies; a box at the beginning of each lesson highlights which writing qualities are addressed.

In our approach to teaching writing, the motivation to revise comes from the authentic writing opportunities. The ability to revise successfully comes from the implementation of the students' Personal Record of Strategies and Skills. The result is writing you and your students will be proud of.

What writers need to know and be able to do:

1. Understand the qualities of effective writing

Purpose: "…that point at which writers concentrate their attention." (Donald Murray)
- Focusing on a topic
- Addressing an audience
- Engaging the reader

Development: "Clutter is the disease of American writing." (William Zinsser)
- Collecting and selecting appropriate details to extend the topic (e.g., examples, explanations, descriptions, arguments)
- Learning what to leave in and what to leave out

Organization: "…a plan—altered according to changing conditions—is essential if the voyage is to be successful." (Donald Murray)
- Finding a format
- Arriving at a conclusion

Language: "The difference between the right word and the almost right word is the difference between lightning and the lightning bug." (Mark Twain)
- Achieving coherence/fluency
- Choosing the right words
- Controlling sentence structure

Conventions: "I choose always the grammatical form unless it sounds affected." (Marianne Moore)
- Using correct grammar and punctuation

2. Learn the techniques and tools of the revision process and use them for real writing for real audiences
- Choosing meaningful writing opportunities
- Revising and editing to apply and use the qualities of effective writing
- Maintaining and using the Personal Record of Strategies and Skills

Defining the Revision Process

The *revision process* involves two distinct aspects: *revising* and *editing*. Revising focuses on purpose, development, organization, and language; editing addresses spelling, punctuation, and grammar. Naturally there is some overlap between the two tasks and differences in approach to the tasks among writers. For instance, some writers leave the editing until the last draft, while others edit as they revise—or vice versa. Explain to your students that these are writers' choices, but that there is no choice as to whether to do one or the other. Good writers work through the revision process by both revising and editing. Whereas our other book, *Grammar Lessons You'll Love to Teach* (2005), dealt with editing skills and grammar, the primary focus of the lessons and strategies in this book is revising for purpose, development, organization, and language.

It is clear that students need time to learn and practice the process of analyzing their work and using revision strategies on their own; therefore, we urge you not to use the revision exercises for grades. Just as batting practice is not applied to one's batting average and practice on the driving range doesn't affect the golf player's handicap, writing and revision practice should count as just that: practice. If things go as planned, no more dark and stormy nights of futile work for you; instead you will be able to celebrate your students' progress as their writing improves throughout the year. And it *will* improve because your students want the rewards of real writing success.

Expanding Your Writing Program: Going Beyond "The Five-Paragraph You-Know-What"

We all agree: Students must want to revise, and not just for good grades. In fact, any writer will want to revise only if he or she really wants his or her writing to be read. This sounds like a simple concept, but unfortunately most of the writing done in schools involves essays on assigned topics. Wouldn't you love to see kids eagerly exchanging papers and avidly reading one another's pieces? Instead, we teachers feel pressured to assign what Tom Romano calls "the five-paragraph you-know-what" because that's the genre required on state and standardized tests (2004). It is the one genre that is easy to grade with a rubric; not surprisingly, more often than not the high scores go to the formulaic and boring essays. No wonder the kids are not eager to revise, much less to have their friends read their writing.

However, we know that expository writing is a useful genre. It's not difficult to teach, and its basic principles can be used in many forms of exposition, including book/music/movie/concert reviews, college essays, SAT II writing, literary analysis, history explications, science projects and lab reports, letters to the editor . . . right on up to resume cover letters and Fortune 500 annual reports.

The challenge, then, is to teach this important genre so that student writers end up with pieces that they want others to read, that they want to see published, and, therefore, that they want to revise before sending out to the world. You can begin by designing essay assignments for real audiences, such as critical reviews, opinion pieces, letters to the editor, and articles for the school newspaper, and require that students submit at least one piece for publication or to a contest in the first term. Watch their motivation to revise go through the roof when they realize that they are competing for the $100 prize in the Creative Communications annual essay contest (www.poeticpower.com) or for publication in *Teen Ink*, a national newspaper and Web site of student writing.

And of course you don't want to neglect fiction and poetry writing in your classroom. Not only is it important to extend expository writing beyond the five-paragraph essay into other nonfiction genres for authentic audiences, but it is also important to emphasize fiction. Real writers read all genres, and so should your students. If we want students to learn to read, write critically, and even answer multiple-choice questions about poems and stories, what better preparation than to write in those genres themselves? In addition, allowing young writers to use mentor writers in fiction and prose promotes practice in eloquence and elegance—qualities we hope they will use in their nonfiction writing as well.

Our Five Basics:
Getting Students to Care About Their Writing

Whether they're writing an essay, a short story, or a poem, you want your students to care about their writing—and therefore to care about revising. With that fundamental goal in mind, we believe each writing prompt and assignment a teacher designs should include the following.

1. **An opportunity for ownership.** Each student should write about a different experience, response, book, event, or product that he or she has experienced and that he or she feels qualified to discuss.

2. **Time.** Students need time to verbalize first opinions, read models, and understand criteria, then write a first draft, revise, self-evaluate, and edit.

3. **Models.** Students should read a variety of exemplary samples of any genre they are required to write in; from those models, they can generate criteria for content and form.

4. **Peer response.** Students should participate in a Writing Circle, to which each student brings a typed copy of his or her writing to read aloud to one or two peers and receive responses.

5. **Authenticity.** Students should have more than one venue for publication or going public with their work.

   - Create a binder in your classroom titled *Class Book* for any pieces students wish to publish. Once writing is submitted to this binder it can be read by anyone in the classroom at any time, which is one form of publishing or "going public" with writing. Be sure students write their name and the title of their piece on the table of contents on the first page of the binder.

   - Set up a file box with folders for your school and/or local newspaper, literary magazine, and any other local publications aimed at kids that accept submissions from young writers.

   - Expand your file box to include publications that reach a greater audience. This idea is so motivational that we include a complete set of steps, How to Go Public, and the reproducible Places to Go Public (see page 14).

How to Go Public

Here are five ideas to help you and your students get started in real writing for real audiences.

1. Subscribe to and display publications that print student writing. Encourage students to submit to the school and the local newspapers, but also to publications that reach wider audiences. See Places to Go Public for a recommended list.

2. Post information about the following contests and encourage students to enter:

    Scholastic Art and Writing Awards: www.scholastic.com/artandwritingawards

    Letters About Literature: www.loc.gov/loc/cfbook/letters.html

    Ann Arlys Bowler Poetry Contest: www.weeklyreader.com/teachers/read/RDContests

3. Print and post home pages of Web sites that publish teen writers and offer resources and lessons. Assign students to explore them, submit writing, experience the lessons, and report to the class:

    www.scholastic.com/writeit (*WriteIt* is part of Scholastic's Web site)

    www.weeklyreader.com/readandwriting (*Writing* magazine's Web site)

    www.merlynspen.org (a pioneering magazine, now a Web site that publishes teen writers)

4. Make it easy for students to submit their writing:
    *   Set up a file box in your classroom with a folder for each of these publishing opportunities. (There is no need for folders for the Web site submissions. Folders for the several publications and contests listed above are plenty to start.)
    *   Allow students to submit by simply putting the writing in the appropriate folder.
    *   Include the publication's submission requirements in each file in a plastic sleeve so that students can be sure to write the submission information on their writing.
    *   Once a month, go through the folders and mail the writing to the publishers.

5. Read these publications and use them to inspire your writing assignments so that they can become writing for real reasons and real audiences.

Places to Go Public

The world deserves to read what you have to say! Go public by submitting your writing to one or more of the publications below—they are looking for writing by teenagers and are eager to publish young writers. Don't forget to revise so that you send your best effort.

Teen Ink (grades 7–12). This Web site, monthly newsprint magazine, and quarterly poetry magazine features personal essays, short stories, reviews (books, CDs, concerts, movies), and interviews from young authors. Include your name, year of birth, e-mail address, home address/city/state/zip, phone number, school name, and English teacher. Include a signed originality statement: Write at the end of your submission, "This will certify that the above work is completely original," and sign your name. Mail to Teen Ink, P.O. Box 30, Newton, MA 02461, or e-mail to submissions@TeenInk.com, or submit to www.teenink.com.

High School Writer (grades 9–12). *Junior High School Writer* (grades 5–8). This national publication is published monthly from September to June. It accepts all genres; however, your school must subscribe to the newspaper. Include your name, your school's name and address, and your year or grade in school. Write at the end of your submission, "This is my original work. It does not contain the words of anyone else without proper credit," and sign your name. Mail to High School Writer, P.O. Box 718, Grand Rapids, MN 55744-0718, or e-mail to writer@mx3.com.

Writing (grades 7–12). Published monthly during the school year, this magazine offers teen writers a lot to read about writing, as well as writing prompts, ideas, writing contests, and places to publish writing, including its Web site (www.weeklyreader.com/readandwriting). Send submissions to writing@weeklyreader.com, or Writing, 200 First Stamford Place, P. O. 120023, Stamford, CT 06912-0023.

Scholastic Scope (grades 7–12). This magazine encourages readers to send their writing of all kinds, including reviews of books, movies, or CDs, and poems, stories, and opinion pieces. Each issue offers a variety of writing ideas and a full page of student writing, titled "Having Your Say." Submit your writing to Scholastic Scope, 557 Broadway, New York, NY 10012, e-mail to scopemag@scholastic.com, or go to www.scholastic.com/scope.

Voices from the Middle (grades 5–9). This magazine for middle school teachers published by the National Council of Teachers of English has a monthly section of book reviews written by students, for students. Your teacher may submit up to five reviews from different students each semester. See other guidelines for submitting to *Voices from the Middle* on www.ncte.org.

Scholastic Art and Writing Awards. This is the oldest, largest, and most prestigious writing contest in the world. The deadline is in January each year. Submissions are accepted in all genres. See details on the Web site for submission requirements: www.scholastic.com/artandwritingawards.

WriteIt. This Web site (www.scholastic.com/writeit) offers the best of Scholastic's resources for young writers. There are lessons, videos, interviews with young writers, and many opportunities to submit and publish your writing on the site.

PART II:
Giving Students the Power to Revise: Setting Up the System

Rewriting is the essence of writing.
—William Zinsser

To get "revision righteousness" flowing in your classroom, you need a cohesive, integrated approach that doesn't take over your curriculum, one that enhances your teaching and empowers students. You've committed to offering meaningful writing opportunities; now it's time to introduce a simple system that guides students to apply revision techniques that will lead them to strengthen their writing. This system mirrors the one we present in *Grammar Lessons You'll Love to Teach* (2005), which focuses on copyediting and proofreading. You can easily use the two systems in tandem, and there is some overlap, but in this book we focus on revision strategies.

The beauty of this system is that it is driven by what your students need, not by the calendar or someone else's ideas about what your students should be doing. This section presents the foundation of the system, the Decoder List of Revision Strategies. This list contains explanations for the revision strategies you teach, organized around the qualities of effective writing we describe on page 10.

Also intrinsic to this system are students' individual Personal Record of Strategies and Skills. As they identify and copy the strategies that they need to work on from the Decoder List of Revision Strategies, each student will develop his or her own personal record throughout the year to target writing needs. You may choose to have students record editing skills on the same sheet; see

Revision vs. Editing

Remember, as discussed on page 11, the revision process includes the distinct tasks of revising and editing. While these tasks often overlap in reality, they are important to sort out and address separately for student writers. When students submit work for Teacher Edit, it is assumed that the teacher will make suggestions and corrections that an editor would make, including revision as well as editing corrections. The lessons in this book focus on revision; our previous book, *Grammar Lessons You'll Love to Teach*, has editing lessons and a Decoder List of Editing Skills. We encourage you to teach both revision and editing, and students can easily enter revision strategies and editing skills on one Personal Record of Strategies and Skills.

Grammar Lessons You'll Love to Teach for more details and the Decoder List of Editing Skills.

Introducing the Decoder List of Revision Strategies

Do you remember the first time you saw those elliptical notes in the margins of your papers, like "word choice" or "focus"? Did you have any idea what to do with them? Did your teacher make you look them up in *Warriner's*? When you finally found out what they meant, did

that even help your writing? Chances are, the results were feelings ranging from confusion and frustration to embarrassment and, perhaps eventually, to resignation. Chances are, too, that not many of your classmates rushed up to the teacher and thanked her. Instead they probably trudged home to make the corrections as quickly as they could in order to resubmit the corrected paper—actually corrected by the teacher, mind you.

As we see it, redlining papers as a way of teaching revision or editing is not a very effective way to help students learn to become better writers. Teachers who redline—simply use a red pen to correct and/or use correction codes—help students make required corrections, for sure, but no real learning is happening. Too often, teachers who simply "correct" student writing are really only providing a form of free proofreading.

More valuable than simply correcting errors is actually showing students where their writing could be stronger and teaching them how to improve it. Thus it makes sense to teach the qualities of good writing along with revision strategies for getting these qualities into student writing. The next logical step is to create a list of the revision strategies that we can refer students to when we see a need in their writing; we call this the Decoder List of Revision Strategies. For instance, after teaching a lesson on imagery and noticing a place where a stronger image would strengthen an argument in a student draft, I can simply write *imagery—word choice* in the margin. The student looks up the code, sees the explanation, remembers the lesson, and revises the writing. This process helps students learn and practice revision strategies.

In the first months of the school year, we work as editors on students' compositions, writing revision codes in the margins and offering explicit suggestions on how to incorporate the revision strategy. We also teach lessons on the qualities of good writing and how the revision strategies and techniques can strengthen writing. All this direct teaching pays off; after a few months, we simply write the codes on student work. Students look them up on the Decoder List to refresh their memories, copy the explanation to ingrain the idea more firmly, and then apply the strategy to their next draft. (This same procedure works for editing skills and can be done at the same time.)

Although eventually we may give a progress grade at the end of each term, based on evidence of learning in the Personal Record, we don't give any grades in the beginning. We just make the necessary editorial notations and make positive comments (including suggestions on where to submit for publication) wherever we can. The primary task at this point is to start paying attention to the most common problem areas, and make a list of, say, the top five to use to generate future lessons.

Note: Although this lesson focuses solely on the introduction of the Decoder List for Revision Strategies, you can modify it slightly and use it to introduce the Decoder List of Editing Skills. We recommend introducing both lists within a short time frame so that students have both immediately available.

Purpose

Students will:

- Become familiar with a user-friendly list of strategies used in the revision process
- Start an individual Personal Record of Strategies and Skills

Materials

- Overhead transparency and class set of the Decoder List of Revision Strategies (pages 22–23)
- Overhead transparency of the Personal Record of Strategies and Skills for Ophelia Heartbeat (page 24)
- Class set of the Personal Record of Strategies and Skills (pages 25–26)

Instructional Suggestions

1. Invite students to list ways in which they make use of a teacher's comments on their written work. Write these on the board. The list might include: "Look for the grade"; "Ask my mother what this means"; "Make corrections on computer and print and resubmit"; "Come for extra help"; "Ask my friend what something means."

2. If no one has included it, add this to the list described above: "Ask for suggestions on how I improve future writing." Elicit what specific activities these suggestions might comprise. Some might include: "Reread old papers"; "Remember my old mistakes"; "Ask my father to correct it before I hand it in." Discuss how practical or realistic these kinds of activities really are. For example, will kids really search out and read over their old papers when revising new ones, and how well do students really learn if they are relying on someone else to evaluate their writing?

3. Explain that today you will be giving them a Decoder List of Revision Strategies that will help them decode the notes you write in the margins of their writing. Tell students that they will not have to learn all of the strategies at once—only the ones that they need to focus on in a particular piece of writing. Each strategy will guide them through a way to revise their work for clarity or coherence.

4. Say that now you will show them how the Decoder List works by giving an example comment from a piece of student writing titled "Pet Sitting Earns Teenager Big Bucks." On the board, draw a vertical line to indicate a margin, and to the right of the margin, write the sentence:

   I've never seen one, but I've heard stories about coyotes in the area and I think they eat cats.

5. Demonstrate for students how an editor (you, the teacher, in this case) would mark this sentence during a reading (a process we refer to as Teacher Edit), writing the word *relevance*.

     I've never seen one, but I've heard stories about coyotes in the area and I think they eat cats.

6. Distribute a Decoder List of Revision Strategies (see pages 22–23) to each student and instruct students to find the code word *relevance*. Use your overhead transparency to help students locate this rule. Have a volunteer read the rule out loud. Say that because this sentence does not relate to the focus of the piece as stated in the title, it should be deleted. Cross out the sentence.

7. Distribute a copy of the Personal Record of Strategies and Skills (see pages 25–26) to each student. Tell students that this tool will help them learn and remember to apply revision strategies. Have them write their names on the top in the space provided. To demonstrate how it works, have them copy onto their record the code word *relevance* along with its explanation. Tell them they do not have to copy anything in the explanation that's in parentheses or italics. As they look for the appropriate code word and description, they will be diving right in to the Decoder List of Revision Strategies and putting it to immediate use.

8. Next, display the student sample transparency of the Personal Record of Strategies and Skills on the overhead so that students can check their work.

9. Instruct students to put the Decoder List of Revision Strategies in their binders in a section for writing. Let them know that they will be putting it to frequent use all year long as they revise their own work.

Developing Each Student's Personal Record of Strategies and Skills

Once students have copies of the Decoder List and have started their individual Personal Record of Strategies and Skills, they are on their way to developing their awareness of the characteristics of effective writing. Now you must get the students into the habit of using these tools and learning from them.

The most effective and efficient way to begin this process is by assigning writing on a regular basis, collecting it, and doing ungraded Teacher Edits. Becoming familiar with students' needs through their writing is the truest way for you to identify the strategies and skills you're going to need to teach. And it's the only way your students can start learning from and applying the strategies and skills they are copying from their own writing.

If you value something you must give it class time, so make sure you offer students sufficient time to practice revising on their own while using their Personal Record of Strategies and Skills, as well as time to copy the strategies and skills from Teacher Edits onto the Personal Record.

Purpose
Students will:
- Continue adding to their Personal Record of Strategies and Skills
- Recognize revision strategies that have been lacking in their writing pieces and start using them in current writing

Materials
- Decoder List of Revision Strategies (included in each student's binder, per previous lesson)
- Personal Record of Strategies and Skills (in each student's binder, with practice entry from prior lesson)
- Recently written short student composition, one per student (a book review or the first two pages of a longer piece would work well); these writing pieces should have been submitted for a Teacher Edit and be annotated, using codes from the Decoder List of Revision Strategies

Instructional Suggestions

1. Hold a class discussion by inviting students to answer these questions:

   a. Why do teachers correct writing?

   b. How do they make corrections?

   c. Who is really learning from this?

   d. Who is really doing all the work?

   Chances are, the answers will resemble the following:

   a. So they can issue grades

   b. Using codes and abbreviations we don't understand

   c. The teacher

   d. The teacher

2. Tell the students that you have decided to give all of this power back to them by putting a moratorium on grades for Teacher Edits for the time being. Remind them of the Decoder Lists, now part of each student's binder. Tell them that these lists will demystify those confusing codes. Promise that this will help them to really learn so they will be able to make meaningful revisions. Their writing will gain power and they will know how to strengthen it.

3. Distribute to each student his or her own teacher-edited piece of writing. Allow class time for students to read the notations, search out the codes on the Decoder List, and copy the strategies and skills into their Personal Record of Strategies and Skills. If they do not finish copying all of their skills, assign the balance as homework. Tell students not to discard anything. Alert them that you will check the skills records and writing pieces tomorrow and answer questions.

4. The next day, collect the Personal Records and student compositions to check how thoroughly each student has recorded the targeted skills. Identify students who need more help completing this task.

5. Write a short, positive comment on each student's Personal Record of Strategies and Skills. Just a few words of encouragement make all the difference, such as "Nicely done," or "Don't worry—I promise we'll have a lesson on relevance and focus next week."

6. Return the Personal Records of Strategies and Skills and the student writing pieces. Instruct students to revise their work, making all corrections on their papers and pursuing any further revisions. Assign a due date to submit final papers and/or go public.

7. As the year goes on, you will need to collect the Personal Record of Strategies and Skills less frequently. You will get to the point where you can just circulate around the room and eyeball the records on a regular basis, collecting them only at the end of each term for a completion grade. However, it is important to allow class time for completion and to check them periodically, or students will just stop working on them.

Using the Personal Record of Strategies and Skills During Revising (Before Submitting Work to the Teacher)

The purpose of this lesson is to help students realize that the process of using the Decoder List is cumulative: Each time they copy a strategy or skill into their Personal Record of Strategies and Skills, they are adding to

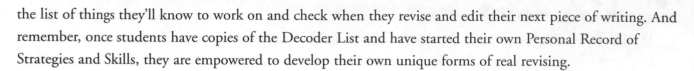

the list of things they'll know to work on and check when they revise and edit their next piece of writing. And remember, once students have copies of the Decoder List and have started their own Personal Record of Strategies and Skills, they are empowered to develop their own unique forms of real revising.

Purpose

Students will:

- Improve their writing by using appropriate revision strategies as noted on their Personal Record of Strategies and Skills
- Develop the habit of maintaining their Personal Records

Materials

- Decoder List of Revision Strategies (included in each student's binder)
- Personal Record of Strategies and Skills (included in each student's binder with entries from an earlier piece of teacher-corrected writing)
- Student compositions, one per student, that have not yet been submitted for Teacher Edit.

Instructional Suggestions

1. Invite students to list the things they do as they revise and edit their writing before submitting their work for a Teacher Edit. Write their comments on the board. Some might include: "I read it over and look for mistakes"; "I show it to my parent/babysitter/tutor"; "I ask a friend to correct it"; "I reread old papers"; "I remember my old mistakes"; or, perhaps, "Nothing."

2. Remind them that they now have a tool that will empower them to specifically target problem areas. This is their Personal Record of Strategies and Skills.

3. Ask students to take out their Personal Record of Strategies and Skills and read carefully the explanations they recorded from their last piece of teacher-edited writing. Clarify any questions students might have about the codes.

4. Tell students that they will now read their most recent writing piece to check only for strategies and skills that they have already recorded in their Personal Records. For example, our sample student, Ophelia Heartbeat, would check her current Personal Record (see page 24) and then read through her new piece to look specifically for ideas or sentences that are not relevant to her topic. With their Personal Records open and available, students should read their compositions with pencils in hand to note places for revision as they encounter them.

5. Students will probably also pick up other errors as they read, but it's best to have them focus at first on previous errors because they will experience real satisfaction if they can catch themselves repeating an earlier mistake and correct it on their own. Circulate around the room and help students make decisions and corrections.

6. Allow students a second chance to read and revise their work, this time reading their writing aloud, softly, to themselves. You might wish to allow them to spread out on the floor to reduce noise distractions, or even spill into the hallway if this is practical. The goal in having them read aloud is to allow them to hear their own words. This will help them to better discern whether their writing makes sense, to catch new mistakes, and to correct stilted or awkward wording.

7. For homework, have students revise and edit their writing and make the corrections they have noted. Tell them to reread the final version aloud one more time to catch any other editing mistakes or typos (especially homonym misspelling and missing words) before submitting for Teacher Edit.

8. Close this lesson by asking students to compose a short list of things they now know they can do on their own to revise and edit their writing. Write the list on the board for them to copy. (You might also copy the list to poster paper and display it on a class bulletin board.) A sample list follows:

> *Things I can do to revise my writing and correct my grammar and usage errors*
> - *Read my Personal Record of Strategies and Skills and then read my writing with a pencil ready to catch the same mistakes and correct them.*
> - *Read my writing aloud, with a pencil ready, and listen for wording and flow.*
> - *After making all corrections and before submitting, read my writing aloud one more time with a pencil ready, looking especially for typographical errors.*

9. Assure the students that as the year progresses and they keep updating and using their Personal Record of Strategies and Skills, they will become much more proficient in revising and editing their own papers. The proof of this will come when they notice that they are being asked to copy fewer and fewer skills after Teacher Edits because of their own growth and progress.

10. As the year goes on, remember to do the following.
    - Frequently remind students that they must copy the skills from Teacher Edits into their Personal Record every time they receive teacher-edited copies.
    - Keep your own running list of strategies and skills that need attention. These will be based on the most common repeated codes that you note and/or appear in students' Personal Record of Strategies and Skills. Plan and schedule class lessons for the most frequent problems.
    - Remember to write a short comment each time you review a student's Personal Record, such as "Good progress—your word choice is really improving!" These comments mean a great deal to students—sometimes they are the only truly helpful and positive things they have heard about their writing.

Decoder List of Revision Strategies

Directions: After you receive a piece that has been teacher-edited, look over the comments and revision notations in the margins of your paper. For each notation locate the effective writing element and the revision strategy that best addresses it. Copy the element and the strategy in your Personal Record of Strategies and Skills (in the Writing section of your binder). Note that the strategy summaries below are meant to be short overviews from lessons, handouts, and notes from class. Be sure to refer to your resources from class for examples of these strategies in real writing.

Remember to consult your Personal Record of Strategies and Skills to revise and edit your next piece so that you use revision strategies to strengthen your writing.

	ELEMENT OF EFFECTIVE WRITING	REVISION STRATEGY
PURPOSE	Focus on a topic	Create a headline or title that summarizes or indicates the main idea and engages the reader.
	Know your purpose	Clarify why you are writing this piece.
	Address the audience	Identify the audience; create a tone appropriate for them; address their concerns.
	Engage the reader	Ask the reader a question; tell a personal story; show how your topic is meaningful to him or her.
	Imagery—tone	Write descriptions of people, places, events, and experiences that reveal your attitude (tone) as well as the atmosphere.
	Choose voice to write in	Write in first person or third person, depending on your purpose; maintain consistent voice throughout.
DEVELOPMENT	Appropriate details and examples	Collect and select details that support your purpose; include relevant examples. Write effective descriptions. Craft a logical argument.
	Relevance	Eliminate details that don't explain your topic or develop the central or main idea.
	3-D characterization	Describe what characters do and what they say; show how other people react around them and talk about them.
	3-D characters—dialogue	Create dialogue that reveals personalities, conflicts, emotions, and relationships.
	Imagery—word choice	Choose words and details that show your readers what you see, taste, touch, smell, and hear.

 Revision Lessons You'll Love to Teach © 2008 by Ruth Townsend Story and Cathleen F. Greenwood, Scholastic Professional.

Decoder List of Revision Strategies (continued)

	ELEMENT OF EFFECTIVE WRITING	REVISION STRATEGY
ORGANIZATION	Format	Choose a format that fits your purpose and topic.
	Organize paragraphs	Focus each paragraph on one topic; within each paragraph, one detail should flow naturally from another.
	Logical conclusion	Arrive at a conclusion that is directly connected to the subject and the details in the paragraphs.
	Coherence—transitions	Use transitional words and phrases (such as *however, then, and, but, yet, next, after, for instance*) and repetition (sparingly) of key words and phrases to show relationships between ideas in one sentence or clause to the next and to show a connection from one paragraph to the next.
	Fluency—importance	Put your most important ideas in independent clauses and the less important but still interesting ideas in dependent clauses or in participial or prepositional phrases.
	Genre conventions	Follow conventions of your chosen genre; use techniques typical of the genre.
LANGUAGE	Concision—word choice	Use specific nouns and modifiers and strong verbs so writing is accurate and focused.
	Concision—appositives	Substitute appositives for lengthy descriptions that are interesting and relevant but not essential to the main idea of a sentence.
	Fluency—avoid choppy or wordy sentences	Avoid short, choppy sentences and long, wordy sentences by substituting single-word modifiers or prepositional phrases or participial phrases to express some of your ideas.
	Fluency—sentence structure	Vary your sentence structures—express some ideas in simple sentences, others in complex or compound sentences.
	Clarity—word choice	Select specific words and phrases that are appropriate for your audience and topic.
	Clarity—images	Choose words that create images and/or describe ideas, feelings, relationships. Avoid nondefinitive generalization (such as *terrific, awesome, great, awful, wonderful*) unless you are quoting someone or creating a character through dialogue.

Revision Lessons You'll Love to Teach © 2008 by Ruth Townsend Story and Cathleen F. Greenwood, Scholastic Professional.

Personal Record of Strategies and Skills

Name: _____*Ophelia Heartbeat*_____

1. Write the date and title of your teacher-edited writing piece.

2. Write each revision strategy code marked on your piece; they will be circled in the margins.

3. Look up each code in the Decoder List of Revision Strategies. Write the revision strategy description next to each code. Put a check next to the code each time your teacher marks it on a piece.

4. Refer to this list to help you revise before you hand in each piece of writing

5. Add to this list each time you receive a Teacher Edit. If you copied the code and explanation in a previous piece but your teacher noted it again on a new one, you must copy the code and explanation again. Note repeats by starring them on this record so that you start to see areas that need improvement.

Date and Title	Code Word/Symbol	Strategy or Skill (use the Decoder List and copy the entire explanation, except examples in italics)
9/10 Pet Sitting Earns . . .	relevance	*Eliminate details that don't explain your topic or develop the central or main idea.*

Personal Record of Strategies and Skills

Name: _____

1. Write the date and title of your teacher-edited writing piece.

2. Write each revision strategy code marked on your piece; they will be circled in the margins.

3. Look up each code in the Decoder List of Revision Strategies. Write the revision strategy description next to each code. Put a check next to the code each time your teacher marks it on a piece.

4. Refer to this list to help you revise before you hand in each piece of writing

5. Add to this list each time you receive a Teacher Edit. If you copied the code and explanation in a previous piece but your teacher noted it again on a new one, you must copy the code and explanation again. Note repeats by starring them on this record so that you start to see areas that need improvement.

Date and Title	Code Word/Symbol	Strategy or Skill (use the Decoder List and copy the entire explanation, except examples in italics)

Revision Lessons You'll Love to Teach © 2008 by Ruth Townsend Story and Cathleen F. Greenwood, Scholastic Professional.

Personal Record of Strategies and Skills (continued)

Date and Title	Code Word/Symbol	Strategy or Skill (use the Decoder List and copy the entire explanation, except examples in italics)

PART III:
Writing and Revising for Real Reasons and Real Audiences

By now you know our philosophy: Students must take ownership of their writing and revising. Our responsibility is to provide them with opportunities to understand the qualities of effective writing and to learn the strategies and skills that produce effective writing. Through experience, we have developed a system that enables our students to learn what they need to know and be able to write for real audiences and enjoy the process. The revision exercises are designed to be fun as well as instructive, just as the writing assignments are designed to address the kinds of writing essential for success in school and, even more important, in "real life." That is why the writing assignments are for real audiences, the only audiences that make us want to revise our writing to be the best it can be.

UNIT 1:
Writing for Critical Analysis and Evaluation

This is the perfect unit to engage your students in writing and revising for real audiences—right after you introduce the Decoder List of Revision Strategies and the Personal Record of Strategies and Skills. The unit incorporates all the steps for writing, revising, editing, and submitting for publication with samples of writing that can be as short as one paragraph, as is the case in Headline News, or much longer, as with Writing a Book Review; it's all dependent on the writer's audience and purpose. You may decide to adjust this assignment so that your students review movies, CDs, video games, or concerts.

Revision Exercise and Writing: Headline News*

If there's one thing about our students we know for sure, it's that they love to talk with one another about themselves—what they did, where they went, whom they met, what they bought, what they saw, what they overheard, etc.—especially on a Monday at the beginning of class. So let's build on that enthusiasm to communicate and generate writing for an enthusiastic, built-in audience by having them write a headline about one significant/interesting event during the weekend and then develop a news story that explains the headline.

Decoder List Strategies

- Focus on a topic
- Logical conclusion
- Concision—word choice
- Fluency—avoid choppy or wordy sentences

Purpose

Students will:

- Focus on a specific topic
- Create a concise, engaging headline
- Develop a short news story
- Use strong verbs and verbals (participles, infinitives, and gerunds) in the composing and revising process
- Write in the third person

Materials

- Transparencies of model headlines (see Step 3 for suggestions, or use your own)
- Short articles collected from newspapers
- Optional: Participles for Lively Writing (page 32)

DAY 1:
Reading, Analyzing, and Writing Headlines

Instructional Suggestions

1. It's Monday morning. You tell your students you know they have things to say to one another about their weekends and you are going to help them do it. They are going to learn how to be reporters who write special feature stories for the class, called "Weekend News." Explain that as they create these stories they will craft professional headlines and write concise news stories in the third person, just as journalists do.

2. Ask students to jot down two or three "events" of their weekend. Assure them that these events might not seem like a big deal, but they can be significant because of something they understood or realized for the first time. Or the events could be action based, such as a birthday party, a visit to a friend or relative, a sports game, a funny incident—whatever was important to them and that they would like to tell their friends about. Give them a few minutes to do this, and you do it, too.

3. Now have students look at their list of weekend events and select one to write about. To begin, they need

*Lesson idea inspired by Erin Ciccone (2001). A place for talk in writer's workshop. *The Quarterly*, 23(4).

to write a headline, which you explain they will likely change later, but for now the headline will focus the topic and jump-start the writing. Of course, you will model the process with some headlines about your weekend, for example:

> Shopping Trip Ends in Near Disaster
> Teacher Confesses to Being Ski-Challenged
> Oscar and Winnie Survive Travel Ordeal

Add some headlines from local and/or national newspapers, especially those from the sports section (sports writers are masters at creating provocative headlines).

> Marching Their Way Into Title Game's Camera
> Hoyas' Defense Smothers High-Powered Irish
> Kicking and scheming, 8 NFL teams in action this weekend
> Embracing Winter Instead of Fleeing It
> Flying to Canada? Better remember your passport
> Tribes' frustrations flare anew
> Feeling at Home Among the Elite
> Giants and Jets Plot a Future Together

4. Ask students, "What do you notice about these headlines?" Answers may include:
   - Most are not complete sentences.
   - There are two different styles (in some the first letter of each major word is capitalized).

   You may have to prompt students to comment on the verbs. Point out *flare, plot,* and *smothers* and ask what these verbs suggest and why the writers used them. Of course, what you want your students to notice is that these verbs create images, reflect deliberate action, and suggest some intrigue—all great ways to appeal to an audience.

   You may also have to point out the frequent use of present participles: *kicking and scheming* (nice play on words), *marching, flying, embracing, feeling.* Participles are called verbals because they're only half a verb; they cannot take a subject, but they can be dynamic adjectives, adverbs, or even nouns, which is why writers, especially sports writers who focus on action, use them frequently. (For specific suggestions for helping students understand the use and value of participles and participial phrases, see page 32.)

   You will want your students to understand that the reason we study these headlines, particularly the choice of verbs and use of participles, is to recognize the economy and power of these language tools for all writers.

5. Now it's time to examine a news story or two to glean the conventions students should use in their drafts. You may choose to display a story on the overhead projector, SMART Board, or monitor, or you may distribute copies to students. Then read the headline and the story aloud. When you've finished, ask students to name the characteristics of writing they noticed in this genre. Guide them to include the following:
   - Use of third-person narrator
   - Answers five W's
   - Brevity

6. Now it's time for your students to revise their headlines and draft the stories that will explain them. (Emphasize the word *draft* because revision will follow; that's the pattern for all our writing.) Remind students to incorporate the characteristics they noticed, in particular writing in the third person, creating professional and catchy headlines, and telling the story vividly but briefly, being sure to answer the journalistic questions of who, what, where, when, why, and how. Allow time for them to do their writing in class, then collect the papers. Don't look at them; just put them away for use in the next class session.

DAY 2:
Writing and Revising Headlines and Stories

The second part of this exercise reviews the qualities of writing discussed in the first part and explores how to revise to include those qualities. You may want to note for students that the revision strategies covered in here all appear on the Decoder List of Revision Strategies. Be sure to tell students that these codes and short descriptions are meant to be shorthand reminders to them to engage in thinking and taking action in these areas of the revision process. Remind them to refer to lessons, practice notes, and handouts done in class on these topics.

The first time you have students do this exercise, you'll want to walk them through the revision process as outlined below. This exercise can be repeated several times; we think of it as a writing workout, similar to practicing plays in preparation for basketball games. Subsequent exercises will not require the explicit instruction, however.

Instructional Suggestions

1. Explain that today's task is to revise the new stories so that they catch a reader's attention (headline) and fulfill the genre conventions of a news story (third-person narrator, answering the five W's). Before students turn to their own drafts, the class will critique and revise a sample news story, at right.

2. Place the sample on the overhead projector, SMART Board, or monitor and distribute copies to each student. Read the sample aloud.

This weekend I earned lots of money pet sitting
My neighbors had to go to a family funeral in Ohio and asked me to take care of their Irish setter Duffy and their cat Ginger. They were going to be away for three days, so I had to feed them in the morning and in the late afternoon. I also had to walk Duffy three times a day and clean out the kitty litter once a day. Ginger likes to be brushed every day, but she is pretty much a house cat. I didn't want to let her out anyway because I was afraid she might not come back in. She could also run away or get in a fight or be attacked by a coyote. I've never seen one, but I have heard stories about coyotes in the area and I think they eat cats. So I made sure Ginger stayed in the house where she likes to be anyway. And I made sure Duffy got three good walks every day. When they came home my neighbors were very happy with the way I took care of their pets, so they gave me $20 for every day they were gone and then a bonus of $20 for doing such a good job. Wow! I got $80 for taking care of animals I like and doing a job that was easy.

(220 words) By Penny Jones

---

3. Invite students to critique, keeping in mind the directions for the assignment, to write the news story as a journalist:

- Write in third person
- Create professional headlines
- Craft concise, focused news stories that tell *who*, *what*, *when*, *where*, *why*, and *how*

4. Help students notice the long-winded headline and use of the first person—neither of these are characteristics of news stories. Then ask students to underline the parts of the story that answer *who*, *what*, *when*, *where*, *why*, and *how*. What they will notice right away is that some of the information in the piece is nonessential, such as why and where the neighbors went, possible outside dangers to Ginger, and the rumors of coyotes.

5. Invite students to revise the piece, working in pairs. In addition to reworking the headline and writing in the third person, inform students that the story is limited to 125 words—that's all the space the paper has for the story, which means students will need to find some economical ways to tell the story. Remind students that this is where strong verbs and participals can come in handy. You'll want to remind them that revising means literally to re-look, to re-vision something. It's not the same as copyediting, when you look for errors in grammar, spelling, usage, and punctuation. Of course, editing is an important part of the revision *process*, but it is not the only part. The revision process also includes real revising that requires writers to think about the purpose of the composition, the audience, the relevance of the details to topic, the logic of the arrangement of those details, and the kinds of sentences and words chosen. That's a lot of work, which is why the writer William Zinsser says, "The essence of writing is revising."

6. After students have worked on revising the story, display the revision below. Read it aloud and ask students to discuss the changes from the original. Some students might say that they like the information about the dangers of the cat being outside, especially the threat of coyotes. The response to that is to ask about the relevance of that speculation to the focus of the story as reflected in the headline. Also, if you have to reduce the word count to about half the original, what details do you delete? What you're doing with this activity, of course, is getting your students to focus on a specific topic and develop it with relevant details presented logically and interestingly—the very essence of good writing.

7. Now it's the students' turn to get to work revising their own headlines and drafts. They may finish their revision for homework if more time is needed.

Pet sitting earns teenager big bucks
Penny Jones discovered this weekend that caring for her neighbor's dog and cat was easy and profitable. The animals had to be fed in the morning and in the evening. Duffy, a friendly Irish setter, needed to be walked three times a day, but Ginger, the cat, was content to stay in the house as long as her litter box was cleaned regularly and her coat brushed once a day. Obviously the neighbors were pleased with Penny's care of their animals because they paid her $20 for every day they were away plus a $20 bonus for doing such a good job. (111 words)

Participles for Lively Writing

A participle looks like a verb, but it's only half a verb, or what we call a verbal. Participles are either in present or past form.

Present participle	Verb	Past participle
cheering	are cheering	cheered
breaking	had broken	broken
eating	was eating	eaten
speaking	is speaking	spoken

A participle cannot take a subject; it must be attached to a verb that can function as a predicate in a sentence. By itself, though, a participle or participial phrase can be a dynamic adjective or an adverb. Sports writers and poets who write about sports use lots of participles and participial phrases. For example:

"The *coaching* genius knows how quickly his reputation can be *tarnished.*"
The present participle *coaching* describes the genius, and the past participle *tarnished* describes his reputation.

"*Screaming with frustration*, the angry fans rushed onto the soccer field."
The participial phrase *Screaming with frustration* adds to the description of the fans.

"Antoine Winfield's *crunching* tackle sent the ball *flying end-over-end toward the end zone.*"
The present participle *crunching* describes Winfield's tackle, and *flying end-over-end toward the end zone* is a participial phrase that describes the motion of the ball.

You have to be careful to avoid the dreaded misplaced participial modifier or you'll end up with some strange, even silly sentences:

- *Hissing and yowling in the tree, the fireman tried to rescue the cat.*
  This sounds like the fireman was hissing and yowling in the tree.
- *The baby was delivered and handed to the pediatrician, breathing and crying immediately.*
  Was the pediatrician breathing and crying immediately? That's odd.
- *The neighbor's lawn mower was reported stolen by the police.*
  Oh my gosh, the police stole the lawn mower! Could that be right?
- *Lying on the beach all day, her mother was afraid Ursaline would get sunburned.*
  How could Ursaline get a sunburn if her mother were lying on the beach all day?
- *Flying over New York City at night, the Empire State Building looked like a welcoming beacon of light.*
  Could the Empire State Building be flying over the city?

The problem with all but the last sentence is that the writers have failed to put the participial phrases close to the nouns they are modifying, so the intended meanings are not stated. In the last sentence, the writer failed to provide a noun or pronoun for the participial phrase to modify, so the phrase is dangling, unattached to anything, unless, of course, the writer meant that the Empire State Building was flying over the city at night.

How would you rewrite these sentences to get the participles where they belong?

Writing a Book Review and Using Revision Strategies

In this series of lessons, students draft and revise book reviews, applying the important concepts and strategies learned and practiced in Headline News, including using strong verbs and verbals and tightening focus by eliminating unnecessary details. In addition, we address arranging sentences and paragraphs for development in a way that is logical for readers.

This lesson is broken up over four days and offers students the opportunity to examine models of successful book reviews and receive feedback from fellow writers.

DAY 1:
Giving Book Talks and Exploring Book Review Techniques

Purpose
Students will:

- Present book talks
- Study models of successful book reviews
- Identify strategies and techniques to use when writing book reviews

Materials

- Books for students to talk about
- Book for teacher to use to model book talk
- Overhead of Book Review Sample 1 (page 40)
- Class set of Book Review Samples (pages 40–41)

Instructional Suggestions

1. A few days before you plan to begin the lesson, tell students to select a book to share with the class and let them know your expectations for the book talk. We ask students to show the cover, describe the book's basic plot/genre in a sentence or two, and include their opinion on what kind of reader might enjoy it. Sometimes we also ask students to give it a rating, based on five stars for "Don't miss it!" to one star for "Not worth reading."

2. On book talk day, bring in a novel that's been popular with students and model giving a book talk.

> Here is the book I chose for our book talk today, *The Outsiders* by S. E. Hinton. As you can see from the cover and the blurb on the back, it's about high school kids who are in different social groups. The kids who live in the wealthier part of town are called the Socs because they are considered more "socially acceptable"; the other kids, not as popular or athletic or economically stable, feel like outsiders. The story lets you into the lives of the teenagers in each group, and you see them clash in different ways. There are moving and exciting incidents of loyalty, violence, friendship, and learning while the main character, Ponyboy, goes through difficult times.
>
> I recommend this book for readers who like realistic fiction and lots of action. The author was 17 years old when she wrote it, and it was an immediate classic.

3. Then go around the room, having each student give his or her book talk. As the students present their books, have a volunteer record a list of titles, authors, and recommendations to post on the bulletin board.

   Right away the students have ownership in choosing the books they recommend to their peers. They have the teacher model the book talk for them and they get responses during class. There is authenticity in the real service they are providing their peers by offering good books to read and posting the list in the classroom for future reference.

4. Express enthusiasm for the books recommended and point out that such recommendations are an excellent way to find new books to read. In fact, readers share their thoughts about books in all kinds of forums—book talks in classrooms, discussion in book groups, and in reviews published in newspapers and magazines. Published reviews have the benefit of reaching a wide audience, and that is the writing task students will try next.

5. Explain that before you begin writing in a genre, it's helpful to examine samples of that genre to get a sense of the appropriate content, format, and conventions, much as you did in Headline News. Distribute copies of the handout Book Review Samples to read as models written by kids, for kids, that have appeared in national publications. If you offer the option of writing other kinds of reviews, add copies of those kinds of reviews. You can find them in *Teen Ink, Writing* magazine, teen magazines, and newspapers.

6. Put one book review sample on an overhead projector, project it on the board, and read it aloud. Have students comment on what they notice about the book review. Jot notes to list the techniques they describe on a blank overhead (or in the margin) as they comment, such as:

   Starter List of Sample Book Review Techniques
   1. Engaging headline
   2. Open with a quote from the book (or use a quote in the review)
   3. Give your opinion
   3. Connect to a recent movie/book/world event
   4. Include a short summary—but don't give away the end!
   5. Use a specific format with book information (title, author, publisher, etc.)

7. For homework, assign students to analyze and annotate the sample reviews. The assignment we give is at right; the directions also appear at the bottom of the Book Review Samples handout.

Homework

Read the rest of the reviews. Annotate each review by doing the following.
1. Underline at least one sentence that includes a technique from the Starter List of Sample Book Review Techniques or a new kind of technique that we did not see in today's sample.
2. Write the technique (such as "engaging headline") in the margin, as we did today on the board. Try to find a variety; if you encounter a new technique, then make up a good title for it, such as "Mention if it's part of a series."

DAY 2:
Drafting a Book Review

Students will now become active in the process of learning about this writing genre and the vocabulary of writers. They will list and discuss book review writing techniques and choose the ones they might use. As a result, as they begin drafting their book review, they will begin to internalize the basic elements of a review.

Purpose

Students will:

- Identify techniques typical of book reviews
- Choose certain techniques to use in their own writing
- Write a concise, engaging book review with a headline
- Use strong verbs and verbals (participles, infinitives, and gerunds) in the composing and revising process

Materials

- Yesterday's overhead listing techniques students noticed from sample review (see Day 1, Step 6)
- Overheads of sample book reviews
- Class set of Book Review Techniques handout (page 42)
- Class set of Book Review Assignment and Checklist (page 43)
- Student homework from Day 1

Instructional Suggestions

1. Distribute the Book Review Techniques handout. Ask students to take out last night's homework. Display the first book review overhead and ask for volunteers to share the labels for different techniques in the review from their homework notes.

2. As the students explain the techniques, underline the passages they are discussing and write the label for the technique (a short phrase) in the space beside it. Check if the technique appears on the Book Review Techniques handout. If not, have students add it to their handout.

3. Repeat this procedure with each review, urging students to come up with different kinds of techniques, as well as noting repeated use of some techniques.

4. Have the students take turns reading aloud the techniques they have added to their lists. Ask the students to put a star next to one or two techniques they think they might want to use in their book reviews, or that they might enjoy reading in a future book review by a peer. Go around the room and have students read one starred technique each.

> Note that all of these steps involve the students in the real work of writers: time (to read discuss, share, understand, and write), models (using a variety of book reviews written by students), ownership (in labeling and choosing techniques), response (in sharing techniques they identified, as well as those they chose), and authenticity (all of these activities, culminating in creating their lists, will help them in the real work of writing their own reviews).

5. Leave time at the end of class to distribute the Book Review Assignment and Checklist. Read it aloud to students. It is very important that they know they will be sharing their book reviews with one another. This gives them their purpose and audience and also gives them fair warning that each student will be expected to write something that he or she is willing to have others read. Assure the students that there will be no peer correcting or grading; they will learn how to respond in only positive and helpful ways.

6. Students may begin drafting in class if there is time.

7. For homework, assign students to write the first draft of their book review. Our directions are at right.

8. As the teacher, your homework is to review the list of book review techniques and determine if you need to type up a new copy with the student additions.

> **Homework**
>
> Write the first draft of a book review (about three paragraphs) that uses at least three of the techniques we have discussed. Bring it to class tomorrow, with the book you are reviewing. You will have time in class to begin revising it.

DAY 3:
Revising the Book Review

Purpose

Students will:

- Recognize audience, purpose, form, and development
- Apply revising skills (for purpose, development, language) and editing skills

Materials

- Book Review Techniques handout (students received this on Day 2, but you may choose to augment the list after students' discussion and additions; page 42)
- Overhead of Book Review Assignment and Checklist (same handout distributed to students yesterday; page 43)
- Students' first drafts of book review (minimum two paragraphs) and class notes/handouts.

Instructional Suggestions

1. Project on screen the Book Review Assignment and Checklist and instruct students to take out their first-draft book reviews. Ask students to share with one another what was difficult for them while writing and what was easy. Encourage participation by asking students for suggestions on how to deal with difficulties others encountered. This will give the students an overview of the assignment criteria/checklist. Give students time to note on their book reviews any ideas for things to add or change on their drafts.

2. Ask students to take out their Book Review Techniques handout. Give students time to read the list and put a star next to any two techniques they might want to use when finishing their book reviews or in future book reviews. Go around the room, asking students to read one of the techniques they chose. Remind students to use this list while finalizing and revising their book reviews for homework.

3. Address the writing quality of organization by suggesting that your students experiment with placement of details and paragraphs. The students should write directly on their book reviews, following these directions.

Experiment with these techniques and decide if they strengthen your writing:
- Choose one detail or element that might not be relevant or essential and draw a line through it. Does this maintain focus by eliminating unnecessary details and/or irrelevant words?
- Bracket a sentence or paragraph that could be moved and draw an arrow to where it could be placed. Does this change make the development more logical for your reader?
- Choose one or two sentences in your review and change a verb to a stronger one and/or use a verbal to make your writing concise and interesting.

Give students a chance to talk about these experiments and any resulting changes they might decide to make.

4. Give students time to revise their book reviews based on their review of the assignment and book review techniques and their experiments. Also encourage students to use the strategies they learned and practiced in the Headline News exercise and any strategies they have noted on their Personal Record of Strategies and Skills.

5. If there is time, have students start revising their book reviews; our directions appear at right. Remind them that they must turn in a revised, edited, typed book review tomorrow for peer response.

> **Homework**
> Use the Book Review Assignment and Checklist, the Book Review Techniques handout, and your Personal Record of Strategies and Skills to revise your book review. Print a copy to bring to class for peer response tomorrow.

DAY 4:
Responding to Peer Book Reviews

Purpose

Students will:
- Respond to one another's writing in nonjudgmental ways that help the writers
- Share their writing with readers
- Consider their readers' comments
- Make notes on final edits and revisions

Materials
- Overhead and two copies per student of Writing Circle Peer Response to a Book Review (page 44)
- Staplers or paper clips
- Overhead of model book review

Instructional Suggestions

1. Explain to students that today they will learn to respond in different ways to their peers. They will be speaking as readers and writers and in ways that will really help one another. We say something like,

When a writer receives a response sheet that has lots of comments and quotes, it feels great. Do this for your classmates and be sure to honor their writing efforts with thoughtful and specific responses to the questions on the response sheets that show you read and appreciated their writing.

2. Distribute the Writing Circle Peer Response to a Book Review, giving two copies to each student. Display it on the overhead and read it over with the class, answering questions and clarifying terms. You might be tempted to skip this step, but it is important. If you don't answer the questions now, they will come up while the students are filling out their own responses, and you will then be answering the same question numerous times and/or interrupting other students' concentration.

3. After reading the sheet aloud and discussing it, model how to prepare helpful responses. Display and read your model book review and ask for answers to each of the questions, guiding students to frame responses in a positive way. As students respond, jot the answers in the spaces on the overhead, completing a sample peer response sheet.

4. Invite the students to discuss how these kinds of responses might be helpful to writers. Support student discussion and emphasize that these kinds of responses really help the writer know what his or her readers got from the piece. They contain invaluable information for writers from their readers—something not all writers get before they submit writing to readers or publishers. At the end of the discussion, we say something like:

Writing Circle Peer Response to a Book Review

Student writer: _Giuliana_   Book title: _Among the Betrayed_

Peer responder: _Ivan_   Date: _Sept. 20_

Student writer's request to responder: Ask a question or write one thing that you would like to learn from your responder:
Is the plot summary too confusing? Is there a certain word or phrase that makes you want to read the book?

Peer responder:

1. Reply to the student writer's request as written above.
The plot summary was not confusing to me, although it does seem to be a complicated and unusual book. I think it helps that you say the book is futuristic in the first sentence, so the reader knows that before reading the plot summary. The title of your review also helped me have a hint of the plot and made me want to consider reading the book.

2. Write two or more words or phrases that stood out while you read the review:
"Lies, deceit, and betrayal . . ."
"But there is a snag – . . ."

3. Describe/name two book review techniques that you notice the student writer included. Include one or two words from the review in quotes to locate the techniques.
a. _mention if the book is part of a series "read this book, the third in the Shadow Children series"_
b. _give the book a rating—"I give this book two thumbs up—way up!"_

4. Write a positive comment (something you admired or noticed about the writing):
I like how your first sentence pulled me into reading the plot summary after it. Also, the summary makes the book sound pretty interesting and exciting.

5. Write a suggestion to submit for publication in addition to Class Book (circle one or more):
(Teen Ink)   Voices from the Middle   High School Writer   (Scope)
other: _Bookworm magazine_ (school/local newspaper, literary magazine, etc.)

At the end of class, when you will receive your responses from peers, you will consider the responses and questions from your responders and decide whether to take action on them. It is *your* writing, so of course you might decide not to change certain things; however, getting the feedback is always helpful, no matter what you decide.

For example, one responder asked the writer, "What kind of virus was it?" The writer decided not to change her review because she really wanted her readers to wonder about that. Another responder asked, "Isn't that by the same author who wrote *The Da Vinci Code*?" The student writer then realized it might be good to add that fact to his review, since lots of his friends had read *The Da Vinci Code*.

No matter what responders say or write, their input gives you valuable information about what your readers will get from your writing. Their input gives you the power to revise to get what you want across to your readers.

5. Collect the students' book reviews and redistribute them so that no student has his or her own. Tell the students to get to work by filling in the spaces on the top for names, titles, and so on, and then reading and responding to the review.

6. Circulate while students are working, encouraging students to include quotes from the writing (words or phrases are fine; they do not have to be complete sentences) and specific elements. Remind students that you will be collecting these responses and reading them, noting the content for classwork effort grades. (You will do this tomorrow when the writers submit their final draft, with this draft and the response sheets stapled to it.) Skim their responses as you circulate so that no one is tempted to write something inappropriate. When a student finishes a response, staple or clip the response to the back of the review and give it to another student who has finished responding. Continue to do this until all reviews have had two responses.

7. If there is time before the book reviews (with responses attached) are returned to their authors, we like to ask the student peer responders to underline one or two sentences that worked well or stood out to them. Then we ask them to take turns reading them aloud to the class. We are always surprised and gratified to hear the variety of writing voices and techniques. It is especially gratifying to the writers to hear their words chosen and read by another student.

8. Allow time to return the reviews so the authors can read the attached responses from their peers. You can be sure they will be eager to read them. For homework, students revise and edit their reviews; our directions appear at right.

    When the reviews are submitted for the Teacher Edit, your task is to read with the eye of an editor and mark the final book reviews, using the codes from the Decoder List of Revision Strategies. When you return the reviews, be sure to allow students class time to read your edits and enter them on the Personal Record of Strategies and Skills.

Homework
- Make revisions and edits tonight based on suggestions of your peers and ideas you had today.
- Print one copy of the final revised and edited review.
- Staple it on top of today's draft and responses to submit in class on the assigned date.

Book Review Samples

The following are book reviews written by students in grades 7–12. They were published in national publications: *Voices from the Middle* (National Council of Teachers of English), *Teen Ink*, *High School Writer/Junior High School Writer*, *Scholastic Scope* . Consider submitting your book review to one of these publications. It's great to share your writing with others and to see your name in print.

Sample 1

Among the Betrayed by Margaret Peterson Haddix. Reviewed by Giuliana Viglione (This review was published in *Voices from the Middle*.)

Living in the Shadows

Lies, deceit, and betrayal are packed into this futuristic novel. Nina Idi is a shadow child—an illegal third child in a society that only allows two children per family. Jailed for a crime she did not commit, Nina begins to lose hope of ever seeing the light of day again. Then a miracle happens. Her interrogator, whom she calls the hating man, gives her the chance to escape. And all she has to do is figure out a way to make three suspected shadows confess. Simple, really.

But it's not easy getting these three to confess. Even 6-year-old Alia refuses to speak of her past. Then, with only 24 hours until they are all killed, a guard is poisoned, and Nina steals his keys and plans her escape. But there is a snag—the other children will slow her down. Should she bring them or not? You'll have to read this thriller, the third book in the Shadow Children sequence, to find out. You will be on the edge of your seat the entire time. I give this book two thumbs up—way up!

Sample 2

And Then There Were None by Agatha Christie. Reviewed by Kyle McGrath (This review was published in *High School Writer.*)

Murder Most Deadly

Can you imagine being stranded on an island with a murderer and one person dying every day? Most likely not. *And Then There Were None* is a fast-paced and exciting murder mystery about an odd assortment of ten people summoned to Indian Island by a host unknown to them all. When the group arrives on the island, their host is nowhere to be found. All of the invited guests have terrible pasts that they are unwilling to reveal. One by one they die, and as each person passes away, one of the ten little Indian figures on the dinner table disappears. The only ones who could not be the murderers are the dead themselves.

I thoroughly enjoyed reading this book. One of the best aspects is that the murderer ends up being the person you would least suspect. I was always on the edge of my seat and engaged in this book. I recommend it to anyone who is a good reader and enjoys fast-paced murder mysteries. I give Agatha Christie's *And Then There Were None* a nine out of ten.

Sample 3

The Da Vinci Code by Dan Brown. Reviewed by Charlotte Kiechel (This review was published in *Teen Ink*.)

Breaking the Code

Renowned curator Jacques Sauniere staggered through the vaulted archway of the museum's grand gallery … The man tilted his head, peering down the barrel of a gun…"Is it a secret you will die for? … when you are gone, I will be the only one who knows the truth." The truth. In an instant, the curator grasped the true horror of the situation. "If I die, the truth will be lost forever…" The gun roared, and the curator felt a searing heat.

In this murder mystery, Robert Langdon is summoned by a French detective. The curator of the Louvre, a most beloved figure in Paris, has just been murdered. On Jacques Sauniere's naked body, strange writing and numbers point to Langdon. Langdon is a professor of Religious Symbology, but now he is brought to the scene, where he is a suspect.

Langdon teams up with Sophie Sauniere, Jacques' granddaughter, who believes in Langdon's innocence. Escaping together, they travel to find the secret her grandfather wanted her to know.

The Da Vinci Code is a fascinating, engrossing mystery with compelling stories of Catholicism, conspiracy, insanity, and secrets that lie in the Bible and Da Vinci's painting *The Last Supper*. I had to read the book in one sitting, and I recommend it to anyone who likes mysteries with twists. *The Da Vinci Code* will keep you scratching your head for days after you have finished it.

Sample 4

Tangerine by Edward Bloor. Reviewed by Alexander Giordano (This review was published in *Scholastic Scope* magazine.)

The Lightning Field

Many people know what it's like to move to a new town, go to a new school, and have to make new friends. In the book *Tangerine*, when Paul's family moves to a strange town in Florida, he is confused about everything that goes on there. The upper school has to have classes in portable trailers, and lightning strikes the same field every day. As Paul settles in, he finds out strange secrets about his older brother, Erik, who is a football star and gets all the attention from his father.

Author Edward Bloor will have your eyes glued to every page. His writing is so descriptive that it feels like his characters are brought to life. You can relate Paul's life to your own. He has many tough decisions to make, just as we do. He has to choose the right friends, the right school, and decide about telling the truth. This is a must-read for people who love realistic fiction with an occasional twist.

Analyze the Reviews

To gain insight into what makes a successful book review, annotate each of the samples:

1. Underline one or two sentences in each review that include techniques that might be used in a review.
2. Label the techniques and write them in the margin. Try to find a variety of techniques.

Book Review Techniques

1. Craft a strong headline.

2. Use strong verbs and verbals.

3. Include a short summary or description that draws the reader into the story, but do not give away the ending!

4. Include a recommendation, such as "Two thumbs up," or "I give it five out of five stars," or "I recommend this book to middle schoolers who like fast-paced mysteries," or "If you like funny books with interesting characters, then you will like this book."

5. Provide basic information about the book, including title, author, and your name and school. You may also include publisher and city, ISBN, price, and number of pages.

6. Indicate the genre, such as thriller, nonfiction, true story, mystery, fantasy, biography, realistic fiction, science fiction, multigenre, or diary format.

7. Write a "grabber" opening—feel free to use "loaded" vocabulary, such as "Lies, deceit, and betrayal. . . ."

8. Ask the reader a question: "Can you imagine being stranded on an island with a murderer? Or a stowaway? But how did he get on? Could crew members be involved?"

9. Mention if the book is a sequel or part of a series (name the series) or movie: "Read this thriller, the third book in the Shadow Children series . . ." or "This autobiography, the basis for the movie *October Sky* . . ."

10. Mention another famous book written by the author.

11. Describe the setting: "It is August of 1768 and the port of Plymouth, England, is bustling with people. . . ."

12. Briefly mention interesting characters.

13. Include a quote from the book that is intriguing, exciting, or interesting: "Renowned curator Jacques Sauniere staggered through the vaulted archway of the museum's grand gallery. . . ."

14. Include your opinion: "*The Da Vinci Code* is a fascinating, engrossing mystery with compelling stories. . . ."

15. Give a personal reaction: "Nick's journal kept me reading for hours on end. . . ."

16. Make a personal connection.

17. Connect to another book or movie.

18. Connect to the world today or to history.

Revision Lessons You'll Love to Teach © 2008 by Ruth Townsend Story and Cathleen F. Greenwood, Scholastic Professional.

Book Review Assignment and Checklist

Assignment: Write a book review.

Audience: Middle school students; other members of our school community

Go Public in: Class Book of Book Reviews (required). Optional: *Voices from the Middle*, *High School Writer*, *Teen Ink*

Form: Typed, double-spaced, 12-point standard font (see samples on book review handout)

Content:

- See samples and refer to your list of techniques for writing a book review.
- Write a minimum three paragraphs, a maximum of five paragraphs.
- Include a short overview of plot and a recommendation for the reader.

Due Dates:

- First draft (at least two paragraphs) due in class on _____
- Complete, typed book review due in class for Writing Circle (peer response) on _____

Checklist for Revising and Editing a Book Review

Format (see models on handout for placement):

- ☐ 1. Title
- ☐ 2. Author
- ☐ 3. Publisher, copyright date, number of pages, price
- ☐ 4. ISBN
- ☐ 5. Reviewed by [your name], grade level
- ☐ 6. School name, city, state

Content:

- ☐ 1. Engaging headline
- ☐ 2. Book review techniques from the models and the list to try new ways of writing
- ☐ 3. Short overview of what the book is about
- ☐ 4. Specific, relevant details
- ☐ 5. Strong verbs and verbals to engage your reader
- ☐ 6. A recommendation for the reader
- ☐ 7. A natural, conversational writing voice with ideas and flow that will engage and interest your reader

Mechanics (do this part last in your revision process):

- ☐ 1. Underline or use italics for the title of a book or play
- ☐ 2. Check spelling and for typographical errors (homonyms, missing words)
- ☐ 3. Check punctuation, including use of quotes
- ☐ 4. Check grammar, especially for fragments and run-on sentences
- ☐ 5. Use present tense when writing about literature
- ☐ 6. Use paragraph breaks to organize your writing

Writing Circle Peer Response to a Book Review

Student writer: _____ Book title: _____

Peer responder: _____ Date: _____

Student writer's request to responder: Ask a question or write one thing that you would like to learn from your responder:

_____

_____

Peer responder:

1. Reply to the student writer's request as written above.

_____

_____

2. Write two or more words or phrases that stood out while you read the review:

_____

_____

3. Describe/name two book review techniques that you notice the student writer included. Include one or two words from the review in quotes to locate the techniques.

a. _____

_____

b. _____

_____

4. Write a positive comment (something you admired or noticed about the writing):

_____

_____

5. Write a suggestion to submit for publication in addition to Class Book (circle one or more):

   Teen Ink   *Voices from the Middle*   *High School Writer*   *Scope*

   other: _____ (school/local newspaper, literary magazine, etc.)

Revision Lessons You'll Love to Teach © 2008 by Ruth Townsend Story and Cathleen F. Greenwood, Scholastic Professional.

UNIT 2:
Writing for Literary Expression

It happens all the time, doesn't it—students bounce into the class excited about a soccer game they've played, a party they went to, a concert they attended, a trip they took, or a special gift they received. You catch their enthusiasm and ask them to tell you about their experiences.

"Awesome," they say, "terrific," "fantastic," "amazing," "wicked funny," "great," "wonderful."

"Oh, yeah?" you ask. "Tell me about it." And then the conversation stops because our students have difficulty getting beyond a sound-bite evaluation of an experience. The problem, of course, is that more often than not they lack the language and the skills to recreate their experiences for others to vicariously enjoy—and for them, the students, to remember and relive for the rest of their lives.

Our challenge as language arts teachers is to enable them to give expression to their experiences and feelings—to "give us the picture" with words as compelling as a photographer's image or an artist's painting.

> **Decoder List Strategies**
> - Clarity—word choice
> - Clarity—images
> - Fluency—sentence structure
> - Organize paragraphs

Revision Exercise and Writing: Sketching With Words

Purpose
Students will:
- Recreate with language an event, a character, an emotion, or a scene from a painting
- Incorporate sensory appeals to enhance descriptions of specific details
- Experiment with diction; with action verbs, specific nouns, adjectives, and adverbs; and with participles
- Recognize and create metaphors
- Vary sentence structures

Materials
- Several art reproductions on transparencies or PowerPoint slides, or on some other medium that allows all students to see the works
- Transparency and class set of Writing Samples of Description: Paintings handout (page 49)
- Transparency and class set of Writing Samples of Description: Narrative handout (page 50)
- Optional: A copy of *The Describer's Dictionary* by David Grambs

Instructional Suggestions
1. Display selected portraits and scenes by famous painters. Hundreds of artworks are accessible via the Internet for you to download, or you may have some art reproductions in your school library appropriate for use in this lesson. You don't need more than three or four pictures, each distinctly different in

style, to stimulate a discussion about what students see in the pictures. Some particular paintings you might select include:

- *Sunflowers*, Vincent Van Gogh
- *The Cheat with the Ace of Diamonds*, Georges de La Tour
- *Nightfall Down the Thames*, Atkinson Grimshaw
- *John, First Duke of Marlborough*, Sir Godfrey Kneller
- *Judith Slaying Holofernes*, Artemisia Gentileschi
- *Between Rounds*, Thomas Eakins
- *The Open Window*, Pierre Bonnard

These are just a handful of paintings from different eras that are dramatic and predictably intriguing to viewers. However, the particular works you select don't matter as long as they are rich in details and engage your students' interest and imagination. You might want to get some background information on your selection by doing a Web search for the title and the painter. We find this kind of information helps students really see what's in the painting, and they find the research interesting.

2. Give your students time to look at each painting, ask questions, and make comments. Then ask the following questions:

- What is the artist showing us?
- What do you think the artist especially wants us to see? What is the focus?
- How does the artist call your attention to certain details?
- What emotions of the people in the painting does the artist reveal or suggest?
- What do you think is the attitude of the artist toward the subject/event being depicted?

Don't hurry through this step—give your students time to look, think, and respond to the questions about each painting. There are no right or wrong answers here; this is an opportunity for students to learn to think about what they look at, rather than simply to glance and then move on.

As your students respond, record their language on chart paper or a transparency so you can save the list. Encourage them to describe every detail that is relevant in the painting, such as:

shapes	light and color	faces	hands	appearance
patterns	climate	heads	feet	
textures	landscape	hair color	manner	
proportions	body type	hair style	expressions	
positions	stature	facial features	dress	

If students are stuck for a word or expression, help them. And if they can offer nothing more than non-specific evaluative words such as *pretty, ugly, messy, mean, nice, beautiful, handsome*, and so on, go ahead and record them. You don't want to stop the initial flow of responses. You can deal with these nonspecific responses later as students study some sample "word paintings."

3. Review with your students the list of language they generated describing what they saw in one of the paintings. Ask, "If you had not seen the painting, from which words and phrases could you draw a picture of something in the painting?" Highlight those specific words and phrases that best describe the painting—and

that contribute to the "word pictures." Here's where you can note that the lack of specificity in *nice, wonderful*, and *beautiful* doesn't help the reader imagine the painting—they don't create word pictures.

You may want to point out that writers, like artists, need to be observers and questioners. Artists communicate what they see and feel with light, color, shape, perspective, arrangement, texture, and volume. Writers communicate with language; they use words to "paint" what delights, frightens, saddens, amuses, hurts, bewilders, stimulates, encourages, fascinates, repulses, and engages them. Being able to give words to the experiences of our lives is empowering—that is what fluency with language is all about.

4. Share samples of brief descriptions other viewers of these paintings have written; see student handout on page 49 for a selection.

5. Discuss with students the writing techniques that help the writers describing works of art to create verbal sketches. Have your students take notes and add them along with the verbal sketch samples to their notebooks for future use. Here is what we point out for the descriptions on page 49:

Between Rounds

Eakins pulls us into the scene to witness the cheers of the crowd, the smell of cigar smoke, and the sweat of the boxer coming from the painting. But the fighter, caught in the few moments between rounds, sprawled on a stool in the corner of the ring, is the focus of the work.

In this brief description the writer appeals to more than our visual sense; he wants us to experience
- "the cheers of the crowd"
- "the smell of cigar smoke"
- "the sweat of the boxer"

These appeals to the senses, along with the description of the fighter "sprawled on a stool in the corner of the ring," allow us, even without seeing the painting, to experience something of the scene depicted.

Sunflowers

Brilliant and startling, this simple vase of sunflowers explodes with razor-sharp vibrancy. The brushstrokes have been laden with thick paint that Van Gogh applied like a sculptor slapping clay onto a relief. The colors—shades of yellow and brown—and the technique express a world of hope and of sunlight.

Here the writer creates a verbal sketch of the details of Van Gogh's painting by using visually stimulating
- adjectives such as *brilliant, startling, thick, yellow,* and *brown*
- noun phrases such as *simple vase of sunflowers, razor-sharp vibrancy, world of hope and of sunlight*
- verbs such as *explodes, have been laden, applied,* and *express*
- varied sentence structures (syntax) such as beginning the description by placing two adjectives, *brilliant* and *startling,* before the subject of the sentence that they modify, *this simple vase of sunflowers*; and in the third sentence, by separating the compound subject, *The colors* and *the technique* with an appositive, *shades of yellow and brown*
- metaphors (comparisons) such as *like a sculptor slapping clay onto a relief,* a stated comparison; and implied comparisons such as *vase of sunflowers explodes with razor-sharp vibrancy*

6. Distribute Writing Samples of Description: Narrative for students to analyze. Divide students into groups of three or four, assigning each group two or three samples. For each sample, groups should identify the language techniques used to sketch an image, an idea, or an emotion.

7. Have each group share its findings with the rest of the class so that all the students can highlight and identify the techniques on their copy of the handout.

8. Invite students to flex their descriptive writing skills by writing their own verbal sketches of paintings. Remind them to incorporate the techniques they discussed in class. We've used the following works with success: *Marilyn Diptych*, Andy Warhol; *Mona Lisa*, Leonardo da Vinci; *In the Car*, Roy Lichtenstein; *The Ball at the Moulin de la Galette*, Pierre Auguste Renoir; *Windows*, Charles Sheeler; *The Battle of San Romano*, Paolo Uccello; *Christina's World*, Andrew Wyeth; *American Gothic*, Grant Wood; *Guernica*, Pablo Picasso; *The Finding of Moses*, Giovanni Battista Tiepolo; *Lobster and Cat*, Pablo Picasso.

As students begin to recognize the power of descriptive language in the writings of others and apply the techniques to sketch their own descriptions of events, places, and people and to express their thoughts, beliefs, and feelings, they will gain new understanding of their world and insight into themselves.

Writing Samples of Description: Paintings

Between Rounds

Eakins pulls us into the scene to witness the cheers of the crowd, the smell of cigar smoke and the sweat of the boxer coming from the painting. But the fighter, caught in the few moments between rounds, sprawled on a stool in the corner of the ring, is the focus of the work.

Thomas Eakins
Between Rounds 1898-99.
Collection: Philadelphia Museum of Art © The Philadelphia Museum of Art / Art Resource, NY

Vincent van Gogh
Sunflowers, 1888,
Collection: National Gallery, © Erich Lessing / Art Resource, NY

Sunflowers

Brilliant and startling, this simple vase of sunflowers explodes with razor-sharp vibrancy. The brushstrokes have been laden with thick paint that Van Gogh applied like a sculptor slapping clay onto a relief. The colors—shades of yellow and brown—and the technique express a world of hope and of sunlight.

Writing Samples of Description: Narrative

His face was profoundly wrinkled and black, like a mask of obsidian. The toothless mouth had fallen in. At the corners of the lips, and on each side of the chin, a few long bristles gleamed almost white against the dark skin. The long unbraided hair hung down in grey wisps round his face. His body was bent and emaciated to the bone, almost fleshless.　　　　—from *Brave New World* by Aldous Huxley

The turbid water, swollen by the heavy rain, was rushing rapidly on below; and all other sounds were lost in the noise of its splashing and eddying against the green and slimy piles.
—from *Oliver Twist* by Charles Dickens

The mountains were covered with a rug of trees, green, yellow, scarlet and orange, but their bare tops were beribboned with snow. From carved rocky outcrops, waterfalls drifted like skeins of white lawn, and in the fields we could see the amber glint of rivers and the occasional mirror-like flash of a mountain lake.
—from *Durrell in Russia* by Gerald and Lee Durrell

There was no possibility of taking a walk that day. We had been wandering, indeed, in the leafless shrubbery an hour in the morning; but since dinner . . . the cold winter wind had brought with it clouds so somber, and a rain so penetrating, that further outdoor exercise was now out of the question.
—from *Jane Eyre* by Charlotte Bronte

Dark spruce forest frowned on either side of the frozen waterway. The trees had been stripped by a recent wind of their white covering of frost, and they seemed to lean toward each other, black and ominous, in the fading. A vast silence reigned over the land. —from *White Fang* by Jack London

No coral snake this, with slim, tapering body, ringed like a wasp with brilliant colors; but thin and blunt with lurid scales, blotched with black; also a broad, flat murderous head, with stony, ice-like, whitey-blue eyes, cold enough to freeze a victim's blood in its veins and make it sit still, like some wide-eyed creature caved in stone, waiting for the sharp, inevitable stroke—so swift, so long in coming.
—from *Green Mansions* by W. H. Hudson

His sister, Catherine, was a slender, worldly girl of about thirty, with a solid, sticky bob of red hair, and a complexion powdered milky white. Her eyebrows had been plucked and then drawn on again at a more rakish angle, but the efforts of nature toward the restoration of the old alignment gave a blurred air to her face.
—from *The Great Gatsby* by F. Scott Fitzgerald

Writing Poetry and Using Revision Strategies

Just as writers can learn how to sketch with words by studying master artists and their work, they can be inspired and learn how to structure and craft their poems from master poets. In this section, you will inspire your young writers to use the master poet Walt Whitman as their personal mentor in their own writing and revising of poetry.

When was the last time your students were asked to write a poem for a test? We hope the answer is never, and thank goodness for that. So far, the creators of state and national testing programs have spared students the cruel and unusual punishment of having to write poetry on demand and then be graded on it. However, we all know that tests often drive curriculum, and thus, because writing poetry is not a task on tests, opportunities for students to write and revise poetry in their classrooms shrink every year.

We also know that this not only denies our young writers chances to build confidence and skills in expressing themselves through poetry, perhaps the most accessible genre, but it also handicaps them when they are asked to respond to poetry or answer multiple-choice questions about poetry on tests. After all, does it not make sense that those who have written poetry might be more aware of the techniques and craft of poems written by others? In addition, those who write poetry become actively involved in the rhythm, language, and stylistic nuances of writing that express meaning in many different and elegant ways. It stands to reason that those who have tried to write elegant and expressive poems will be more likely to be able to write elegant and expressive expository pieces and test essays as well.

Perhaps the best reason for teaching poetry writing is that most kids prefer writing poetry to any other genre. They all love music, and when they discover that the song lyrics printed inside their CD cases are also poems, they start seeing how poetry is written and used by more than just dead poets and English teachers. Students deserve to know that poetry is a very important part of their lives and a powerful tool that they can use for self-expression, enjoyment, and even in effecting change in their world.

DAY 1:
Learning From Models and Drafting Poems

Purpose
Students will:
- Understand the forms and structures of free verse
- Create verbal images and metaphors
- Write free verse to react to an event, express an emotion or a belief, or create a scene

Materials
- Overhead of excerpts from "Song of Myself," page 57 (class set of copies for students is optional)

Instructional Suggestions
1. Write on the board: *Why do people write poetry?* Elicit comments from students and write the key phrases on the board as they volunteer their ideas, which might include:
   - to express themselves

- for entertainment of others
- to send a message
- for enjoyment of others/self
- to turn into a song
- to tell a story in a freer way
- for publication

Conduct a brief discussion of the uses of poetry, and be sure to point out that the lyrics of most songs, including current ones, are poetry. You might also want to mention the subversive power of poetry to change lives or politics, the narrative possibilities of poetry to memorialize events, and the possibilities that poetry offers to those who feel constricted by prose. This will bring you to the next topic of what poetry is.

2. Write a new question on the board: *What is poetry?* Record student responses, which might include:

Poetry
- rhymes (or not)
- has stanzas (or not)
- creates images
- is sometimes hard to understand
- does not have to be hard to understand
- expresses emotions or feelings or an idea
- has a rhythm
- can be song lyrics
- looks like poetry—has a shape, a form, on the page
- is usually shorter than prose pieces
- is sad/funny/powerful/shocking/meaningful/random/precise/patterned/free

Ask students what they like about poetry, what kinds of poetry they like, what they like to do with poetry. Encourage the discussion to cover the ideas that poetry does not always have to rhyme and does not always have to be difficult to understand, but that it can be a powerful form of communication for them as writers. Tell students that today they will be reading some famous poetry and drafting some of their own, using what they have read as models and inspiration.

3. Give the students a little background on Walt Whitman as a groundbreaking poet of his time, writing in free verse as well as traditional. Explain that one of his most famous pieces is "Song of Myself," an epic poem within *Leaves of Grass*, a cohesive collection of free-verse poems in which Whitman celebrates himself as an integral part of the world.

4. Display the excerpts from "Song of Myself" and read them aloud. After the first reading, ask students what words or phrases stood out to them, and underline them on the transparency. Ask what words they are not sure of, and clarify definitions as well. Discuss the free-verse nature of the writing, and how the lines break in different places—some at a punctuation point, some in the middle of a thought, and so on.

5. Ask for a student volunteer to read the poetry aloud again, and ask students to watch for the ways Whitman is celebrating himself: the specific actions, images, and connections. After the reading, elicit their responses, underlining the words or phrase as they are offered.

6. Tell the students that now they will have a turn to write and celebrate themselves, using Walt Whitman as their mentor. Instruct them to write at the top of their page: "I Celebrate Myself," and, underneath that, "Inspired by Walt Whitman's 'Song of Myself.'" All writers do this when using the work of others for inspiration. Direct the students to do a five-minute quick-write or free-write, celebrating themselves. You may offer the following suggestions to help them get started:

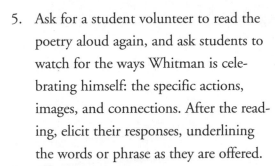

Tip

Use the excerpt below as an overhead the day students begin to write their poems.

The Golden String
Long enough have you dreamed contemptible dreams,
Now I wash the gum from your eyes,
You must habit yourself to the dazzle of the light and of every moment of your life.
Long have you timidly waded, holding a plank by the shore,
Now I will you to be a bold swimmer,
To jump off in the midst of the sea, and rise again and nod to me and shout, and laughingly dash with your hair.
— Walt Whitman, "Song of Myself"
(lines 1225-1230)

- Borrow a word or phrase from the poem to get started, such as "I celebrate myself" or "I too am not a bit . . ."
- Include the specifics from your lives at home, in school, or in other settings.
- Be as free as Whitman to "sound my barbaric yawp" as much as you want.
- Start writing and keep writing for five minutes, with no concern for spelling, punctuation, or grammar concerns. Try to fill the page.
- Write in prose or in a kind of shaped, poetic form, but do not focus on crafting shape at this point in time.

7. At the end of the time, tell students that they will now practice some of the skills they learned in prior revision lessons, such as Sketching With Words. Ask students to do the following:
- Circle every verb and noun, then consider whether there might be a more evocative or precise word or phrase that would create more vivid imagery. If so, students should insert those more evocative or precise words and phrases into the draft.
- Underline all adjectives and adverbs, then consider if each one is necessary or could be eliminated—after all, if the verbs and nouns are strong, modifiers are not always necessary and can clutter poetic imagery.

8. At this point, take the opportunity to have a celebration of your students' poetic selves. Ask students to underline one or two lines of their writing to share with the class. Then go around the room, and invite each student to read his or her lines aloud.

9. Assign students to finalize their poems, using the revision strategies they have learned. Instruct them to bring their complete poems to class the next day.

10. Conclude by sharing the following quote from Whitman; we also display it on an overhead at the end of the lesson.

> *Great is today and beautiful,*
> *It is good to live in this age…there never was any better.*
> —Walt Whitman, "Great Are the Myths" (lines 7–8)

DAY 2:
Revising Poetry for Line Breaks and Stanzas

Purpose

Students will:

- Identify poetic techniques such as enjambment, line breaks, and use of stanzas
- Revise and craft their poetry

Materials

- Transparency of Line Break Experiments: Three Versions (page 59)
- Students' "I Celebrate Myself" poems (homework from Day 1)
- Class set of Line Break Experiment handout (page 60)

Instructional Suggestions

1. Display the Line Break Experiments transparency, covering up all but Version 1 of "Song of Myself." Read that version aloud to the class as they view it. Allow students to comment on this version, since they might notice that it is visually different from the one they worked with yesterday. Ask the students:
   - What lines stand out in this version?
   - What is the structure of the poem? (two tercets, or three-line stanzas, each followed by one line; then a final four-line stanza, or quatrain)
   - How does the structure affect the poem for the reader? Which ideas or lines stand out more than others because of the line breaks and stanza breaks?
   - Where do line breaks occur in the middle of a thought? (They happen on almost every line, and especially in the first line of each stanza. This is using the technique of enjambment, the running over of a sentence from one line into another, so that closely related words fall on different lines.)
   - How does the use of enjambment affect the reader and/or the pace of the reading? (The unexpected line break, or enjambment, influences readers to pause slightly before going to the next line, making some readers wonder what will come next, or even project what will come next. What does come next is then heightened in its intensity because of surprise or satisfaction in the reader.)

2. Cover Version 1 and reveal Version 2. Read this version aloud, making sure to pause slightly at each line break and stanza.

3. Guide students to discuss the second version by asking:

- How does the structure of Version 2 look different from Version 1? (The poem seems shorter because it has fewer lines and is only one stanza. There is no white space breaking up the poem.) Be sure to confirm to them that it is exactly the same poem as Version 1, except for the line and stanza breaks.

- What word or line stands out in this poem? (Most students will identify the last word, *you*, which is alone in the last line.)

- In what other ways is this poem different from the first? (Uncover Version 1 at this point.) Allow students to compare both visually.

Encourage students to make observations and offer opinions on:

- How each version looks different on the page

- How the line breaks and stanzas offers various rhythms and ways to emphasize different words, phrases, and ideas

- How the white spaces in Version 1 separate the stanzas, get readers to pause and gather their thoughts, and slow down the reading of the poem

Be sure to mention that all of these techniques are just techniques—not do's or don'ts, or rights or wrongs. They are tools that poets consciously use to get the meanings they want across to their readers.

4. Reveal Version 3 and allow students to see all three versions at once. Explain that this is Whitman's version. Invite students to:

   - Speculate why Walt Whitman chose to structure the poem in three stanzas and insert line breaks at points of punctuation.

   - Discuss which version they would have chosen if they had written this poem—and why.

5. Challenge students to revise and craft their own poems, using the techniques they examined in these lessons. As homework (see box at right) assign them to type up their "I Celebrate Myself" poems and create three different versions, using different line breaks and stanzas, as directed on the Line Break Experiment handout.

Tip

Another suggested overhead, this time to be shown prior to revising.

Great is language . . . . it is the mightiest of sciences,
It is the fulness and color and form and diversity of
    the earth . . . . and of men and women . . . . and of all
        qualities and processes;
It is greater than wealth . . . . it is greater than buildings
    or ships or religions or paintings or music.

—Walt Whitman, "Great Are the Myths" (lines 41–43)

Homework

Revise your poem, using the revision techniques discussed in class. Then do the Line Break Experiment with your revised poem, following the directions on the handout. Bring in your final poem, along with the one-paragraph explanation about the results of the experiment. We will have a Writing Circle on the poems during our next session.

DAY 3:
Responding to Poems

Purpose

Students will:

- Follow Writing Circle procedures
- Complete the Writing Circle Peer Response form

Materials

- Overhead and class set of Writing Circle Peer Response to a Poem (page 61)

Instructional Suggestions

This stage of the writing process is described fully on pages 37–39; here is a brief outline of the steps.

1. Remind students that they will be responding as readers and writers in ways that will really help one another. Tell them again:

    > When a writer receives a response sheet that has lots of comments and quotes, it feels
    > great. Do this for your classmates and be sure to honor their writing efforts with thoughtful
    > and specific responses to the questions on the response sheets that show you read and
    > appreciated their writing.

2. Distribute Writing Circle Peer Response to a Poem (one copy to each student). Put it on the overhead projector and read it over with the class, answering questions and clarifying terms.

3. Collect the students' poems and redistribute them so that no student has his or her own poem. Tell the students to read the poem and complete the response thoughtfully.

4. Allow time to return the poem with responses so the authors can read the attached responses from peers. Assign students to make revisions and edits tonight based on suggestions from their peers and ideas they had today; they will submit their poems with all drafts and peer responses attached to the teacher for a Teacher Edit.

Excerpts from "Song of Myself" by Walt Whitman

1

I celebrate myself,
And what I assume you shall assume,
For every atom belonging to me as good belongs to you.
I loafe and invite my soul,
I lean and loafe at my ease . . . . observing a spear of summer grass.

10

Alone far in the wilds and mountains I hunt,
Wandering amazed at my own lightness and glee,
In the late afternoon choosing a safe spot to pass the night,
Kindling a fire and broiling the freshkilled game,
Soundly falling asleep on gathered leaves, my dog and gun by my side.

The Yankee clipper is under her three skysails . . . . she cuts the sparkle and scud,
My eyes settle the land . . . . I bend at her prow or shout joyously from the deck.

The boatmen and clamdiggers arose early and stopped for me,
I tucked my trowser-ends in my boots and went and had a good time,
You should have been with us that day round the chowder-kettle.

21

I am the poet of the body,
And I am the poet of the soul.

The pleasures of heaven are with me, and the pains of hell are with me,
The first I graft and increase upon myself . . . . the latter I translate into a new tongue.

(continued)

Excerpts from "Song of Myself" by Walt Whitman (continued)

52

The spotted hawk swoops by and accuses me . . . . he complains of my gab and my loitering.

I too am not a bit tamed . . . . I too am untranslatable,
I sound my barbaric yawp over the roofs of the world.

The last scud of day holds back for me,
It flings my likeness after the rest and true as any on the shadowed wilds,
It coaxes me to the vapor and the dusk.

I depart as air . . . . I shake my white locks at the runaway sun,
I effuse my flesh in eddies and drift it in lacy jags.

I bequeath myself to the dirt to grow from the grass I love,
If you want me again look for me under your bootsoles.

You will hardly know who I am or what I mean,
But I shall be good health to you nevertheless,
And filter and fibre your blood.

Failing to fetch me at first keep encouraged,
Missing me one place search another,
I stop somewhere waiting for you

Line Break Experiments: Three Versions

Excerpt from "Song of Myself" by Walt Whitman

Version 1: Not Walt Whitman's line breaks and stanzas

I bequeath myself to
the dirt to grow from the grass I love,
If you want me again

look for me under your bootsoles.

You will hardly
know who I am or what I mean,
But I shall be good health to you nevertheless,

And filter and fibre your blood.

Failing to
fetch me at first keep encouraged,
Missing me one place search another,
I stop somewhere waiting for you

Version 2: Not Walt Whitman's line breaks and stanzas

I bequeath myself to the dirt to grow from the grass I love,
If you want me again look for me under your bootsoles.
You will hardly know who I am or what I mean,
But I shall be good health to you nevertheless,
And filter and fibre your blood.
Failing to fetch me at first keep encouraged,
Missing me one place search another,
I stop somewhere waiting for
you

Version 3: Walt Whitman's line breaks and stanzas

I bequeath myself to the dirt to grow from the grass I love,
If you want me again look for me under your bootsoles.

You will hardly know who I am or what I mean,
But I shall be good health to you nevertheless,
And filter and fibre your blood.

Failing to fetch me at first keep encouraged,
Missing me one place search another,
I stop somewhere waiting for you

Line Break Experiment

Task: Experiment with one of your poems to create three different versions, a final, fourth version, and a short explanation of your process.

1. Choose one of your poems, preferably one that does not use an end-rhyme scheme or a set rhythm/meter.

2. Copy it three times on the computer, and label them Version 1, Version 2, and Version 3.

3. Change Version 2 and Version 3, using different line breaks and stanza breaks on each.

   Line breaks: Play with line breaks (each line break makes the reader pause and think a bit), word placement and spacing, and the white space. Craft your writing to enhance meaning for your reader.

   Stanzas: Play with stanzas. Decide what to put in each stanza. Craft the shape of your poem to enhance meaning for your reader.

4. Look over all three experiments, decide which changes make your poem stronger, and type a final, fourth version.

5. Type a short, one-paragraph explanation of what you did to get to your final version and why you did it. Be sure to explain what you hope will stand out and/or get across to your reader as a result of your changes.

 Revision Lessons You'll Love to Teach © 2008 by Ruth Townsend Story and Cathleen F. Greenwood, Scholastic Professional.

Writing Circle Peer Response to a Poem

Student writer: _____ Poem title: _____

Peer responder: _____ Date: _____

Student writer's request to responder: Ask a question about something you'd like to learn from your responder.

_____

_____

Peer responder:

1. Reply to the student writer's request as written above.

    _____

    _____

2. Copy any two phrases or lines that create verbal images (words that appeal to any of the five senses: taste, touch, smell, hearing, or sight).

    _____

    _____

3. Copy a phrase or a line that uses a simile or metaphor.

    _____

    _____

4. Copy two words or phrases that offer details that explain or develop the central message or metaphor.

    a. _____

    b. _____

5. Copy a phrase or line that offers vivid word choice and/or is very strong in your memory.

    _____

6. In your own words, write a sentence that describes what the poem is saying to the reader.

    _____

7. Suggest where this poem should go public (circle): *Teen Ink*, Scholastic contest; *Writing* magazine; *High School Writer*; school newspaper/literary magazine; other: _____

8. Add a positive comment or compliment. _____

UNIT 3:
Writing for Literary Analysis and Social Interaction

Our students expect us to ask them to read books and write an analysis, a task that's a challenge even for a professional critic, so it's no wonder our students groan just at the thought of having to "write about the book." Whatever pleasure they may have had from reading the book dissolves at the thought of writing about it. Our task, then, is to create real writing assignments that will engage our students as well as provide them with opportunities to hone their critical reading skills and develop their writing and revising skills.

> ## Decoder List of Revision Strategies
>
> - Relevance
> - Concision—word choice
> - Concision—appositives
> - Fluency—avoid choppy or wordy sentences
> - Fluency—sentence structure
> - Clarity—word choice
> - Clarity—images
> - 3-D characterization
> - Imagery—word choice

Revision Exercise and Writing: One-Sentence Stories*

Imagine announcing to your students that they are going to write a story in only one sentence. In fact, they're going to write several one-sentence stories.

"Oh, sure," one student will say. "You can't write a whole story in one sentence."

"You can, if you know how," you say.

"Yeah, with a whole bunch of run-ons," another says. "That's something you always snag us for."

You assure them they can write interesting narratives in a single sentence, some relatively short, others long. The point in either case is to relate an incident, an event, even a revelation in a single sentence without it being a run-on or a string of short, choppy sentences connected by *and* or some other conjunction.

You promise to show them how to do it while having fun in the process, and as a result be much better equipped to compose and revise their "real writing," like essays, conventional stories, poems, letters, and so on. And that's the whole point of this revision exercise.

Purpose

Students will:

- Create mini-narratives in one sentence, using dependent clauses and prepositional and participial phrases
- Use commas, colons, semicolons, dashes, and parentheses appropriately and correctly
- Understand the value of grammar in drafting and especially in revising

Materials

- Overhead transparency and class set of Parts of the Sentence (page 65)
- Class set of One-Sentence Stories (page 66)
- A collection of "super sentences" as story starters

*Note: Inspired by Don and Jenny Killgallon's book *Sentence Composing* (2000).

Instructional Suggestions

1. Introduce the assignment: to tell a story in one sentence. To help students understand how this can work, model the process of writing a one-sentence story for them by beginning with a "super sentence," which suggests all kinds of possibilities for developing a story. You might use this one: "The king died and then the queen died of grief."

2. Ask students to consider these questions:

   - What might happen to the kingdom now that there's no king or queen?
   - Were there any children to rule the kingdom?
   - What kinds of problems do these two deaths suggest to you?
   - How did the king die?

   Your students may come up with other questions, whose answers can become part of the story. The point is that you (and they) can see how this scaffolding device, the super sentence, can lead a writer to develop a story. Model one way to develop your sample super sentence:

   The king died and then the queen died of grief, leaving a young son, the only heir to the throne, subject to the guardianship of the ambitious and powerful Duke of Blackwole, who conspired with the evil Earl of Savage to smother the little prince while he slept.

3. Distribute the Parts of the Sentence handout and display it. Then walk students through the development of your one-sentence story, showing how you used the following language tools.

   - **Participial phrases:** leaving a young son, the only heir to the throne, subject to the guardianship of the ambitious and powerful Duke of Blackwole
   - **Prepositional phrases:** to the throne, to the guardianship, of the ambitious and powerful Duke of Blackwole, with the evil Earl of Savage
   - **Dependent clauses:** who conspired with the evil Earl of Savage, while he slept
   - **Infinitive phrase:** to smother the little prince

   Point out to your students that without the independent clause *The king died and then the queen died of grief,* the phrases and dependent clauses would be dangling grammatically and also logically because the reader would not understand how the boy prince came under the control of the Duke, who had had the king killed.

4. At least one of your students will probably ask if writers really think about all "this grammar stuff"—these parts of the sentence—when they are writing. And that's a good question, because it gives you the opportunity to explain that experienced writers usually aren't conscious of the specific grammatical structures they're using when they're drafting, partly because they work with the tools of their craft all the time, so they've internalized the process. They hear in their heads the sounds of the language and feel the pace of the narrative. It comes with practice, just as you have internalized some moves on the tennis court or the soccer field or the dance floor. But if you want to improve your game, you will deliberately be conscious of the moves you are making in order to correct mistakes or learn new moves. Writers do the same thing when they are revising their drafts; then they make *conscious* choices as to how to most effectively tell the story.

5. Tell students that now you will share some one-sentence stories written by published authors, to explore how they work and why a writer might choose to use them. Distribute copies of One-Sentence Stories.

6. As you and your students read these sample one-sentence stories, point out how the trailing verb phrases and dependent clauses develop the "story" and pull us into the action. Your students may wonder why Ron Rash describes the drowning of this young girl in only one sentence, but as you read it aloud to them, they will understand the writer's desire to pull us into the urgency and horror of the event. Encourage students to discuss why they think the writers used one-sentence stories.

7. Now your students are ready to create their own one-sentence stories, but first they need to create or select a super sentence to develop. The following list of sentences can be useful for your students to use as starters for their stories or as models to inspire them to create their own super sentences to develop into one-sentence stories:

> The snow began to fall.
>
> Jake gave his mother flowers.
>
> Lorna was terrified.
>
> Quinn broke the small vase.
>
> Grandfather was angry.
>
> The water rose around them.
>
> Maria never liked snakes.
>
> His old car finally died.

8. Give your students some time (not too much) to compose their stories, but add a note of caution: Making a sentence longer does not necessarily make it better. Just adding irrelevant phrases or repeating information in another way makes a sentence redundant and boring. To avoid those pitfalls, students must think carefully about the story they want to tell, the action they want to describe, the scene they want to create, the mood they want to convey—and how to do it all in one sentence, which can, with the right choice of words and skillful use of trailing verb phrases, be short.

Note: During drafting, some students may need the freedom to use a number of sentences just to maintain the flow of the narrative. These students can revise their piece later into a one-sentence story.

If you do this exercise with your students a few times, perhaps as a regular warm-up activity, you'll begin to see prepositional and participial phrases and dependent clauses used appropriately in all their writing. As a bonus you will have a collection of one-sentence stories to serve as models in the future. In any event, we guarantee that students will always be eager to share their "stories" and will actually be writing to entertain one another—and you.

Student Samples of One-Sentence Stories

Proudly Jake presented his mother flowers, a beautiful bouquet of little yellow blossoms, for her birthday, an occasion she wanted to ignore, but Jake didn't know that; he knew only that she seemed sad and thought the flowers would make her smile—instead they made her sneeze and blow her nose.

Her second-hand car had served her well for over twenty-five years ferrying her children to music lessons and play-dates, sleepovers and sports practices, summer camp and family vacations, college tours and graduations—and now she was saying farewell to her faithful traveling companion who finally died.

The snow began to fall in the night and continued until noon when it finally subsided just as Annie awoke from her morning nap, stretched and trotted to her door, rested and ready to chase the chipmunks, climb a tree or two, and scatter the nesting birds, but when she pushed through the kitty door she stepped into mounds of snow so deep she could barely move through it and so cold that the warm pleasure of inside sent her right back through the door, saving the pleasure of outside for a sunny day.

Parts of the Sentence

1. The **predicate** shows action (*swooped, screamed, twitters*) or a state of being (the verb *to be* in any of its forms: *is, am, are, was, were*). It includes the main verb and any helping verbs (*leaps/is leaping; snarled/had snarled*) along with any modifiers that describe the main verb and helping verbs.

   pred.   pred.
   The bird <u>screamed</u>. The lion <u>had snarled</u> at it.

2. The **subject** is the main noun or a pronoun and any modifiers that describe the main noun or pronoun. The predicate tells what the subject does or is. To find the subject, ask *who* or *what* before the verb.

   subj.
   <u>Louisa</u> read that book all day long.

3. The **object** completes the predicate.
   - To find the **direct object**, ask *whom, who,* or *what* after the predicate.

     dir. obj.
     Igor dropped his <u>backpack</u> on the chair.
   - The **indirect object** tells to whom or to what the action of the predicate was done. To find the indirect object, ask *to whom* or *to what* after the predicate.

     indir. obj.
     Luca gave the <u>cat</u> a special treat.
   - The **subject complement** completes the linking verb predicate. Linking verbs are the verb *to be* and verbs of the senses, such as *smell, sound, taste, feel, look, seem, appear, become.*

     subj. comp.
     Tasha looked <u>happy</u> at her birthday party.

4. A **phrase** is a group of words without a subject or a predicate. There are several kinds of phrases, including:
   - **prepositional phrases**, which always begin with a preposition: *to the store, from school*
   - **participial phrases**, which begin with a participle (verb + *-ing* or verb + *-ed*): *walking backward; unconcerned with*
   - **infinitive phrases**, which always begin with an infinitive (*to* + a verb): *to go, to care*

5. A **clause** is a group of words with a subject and a predicate. Clauses can function as subjects, objects, adjectives, or adverbs. There are both:
   - **independent clauses**, which stand alone as complete sentences:

     indep. clause   indep. clause
     <u>The lion snarled</u> and <u>the bird screeched</u>.
   - **dependent clauses**, which must be attached to an independent clause:

     indep. clause   dep. clause
     <u>The bird screeched</u> <u>because the lion snarled</u>.

Note: These simple definitions are reminders; be sure to refer to your grammar book for more detailed definitions and explanations of the parts of sentences.

One-Sentence Stories

Missy was what everyone called me, not that it was my name, but because when I was three supposedly I stamped my foot and told my own mother not to call me Marietta but Miss Marietta, as I had to call all the people including children in the houses where she worked Miss this or mister that, and so she did from that day forward. —from *The Bean Trees* by Barbara Kingsolver

Our house burned in March and we lived that spring in the smokehouse, sleeping in two beds pushed close into the corners, and with strings of peppers and onions hanging from the rafters overhead. —from *River of Earth* by James Still

The people of the village began to gather in the square, between the post office and the bank, around ten o'clock; in some towns there were so many people that the lottery took two days and had to be started on June 26th, but in this village, where there were only about three hundred people, the whole lottery took less than two hours, so it would begin at ten o'clock in the morning and still be through in time to allow the villagers to get home for noon dinner. —from "The Lottery" by Shirley Jackson

She rises coughing up water, gasping air, her feet dragging the bottom like an anchor trying to snag water-logged wood or rock jut and as the current quickens again she sees her family running along the shore and she knows they are shouting her name though she cannot hear them and as the current turns her she hears the falls and knows there is nothing that will keep her from it and the current quickens and quickens and another rock smashes against her knee but she hardly feels it as she snatches another breath before the river pulls her under and she feels the river fall and she falls with it as water whitens around her and she falls deep into darkness and as she rises her head scrapes against a rock ceiling and all is black and silent and she tells herself don't breathe but the need grows inside her beginning in the upper stomach then up through the chest and throat and as that need rises her mouth and nose open at the same time and the lungs explode in pain and then the pain is gone along with the dark as bright colors shatter around her like glass shards, and she remembers her sixth-grade science class, the gurgle of the aquarium at the back of the room that morning the teacher held a prism out the window so it might fill with color, and she has a final, beautiful thought—that she is now inside that prism and knows something even the teacher does not know, that the prism's colors are voices, voices that swirl around her head like a crown, and at that moment her arms and legs she did not even know were flailing cease and she becomes part of the river. —from *Saints at the River* by Ron Rash

Writing a Letter to an Author and Using Revision Strategies

There is nothing like the thrill of getting mail . . . or winning a contest. In this unit, students write letters to authors, and if they choose to send them, they stand a good chance of getting an answer in the form of a letter from their author or perhaps notification of winning the Letters About Literature contest.

Of course, you may have students write letters to authors at any time. However, it's a powerful motivator for students who want to write to dead authors to know that their writing can still be read by a real audience if they enter the contest.

The Letters About Literature contest is an annual event with a deadline in the first week of December, sponsored by the Library of Congress Center for the Book. Students in grades 4 through 12 are invited to write a letter to an author, dead or alive, "explaining how that author's work somehow changed the reader's view of the world or self." The contest has a helpful Web site with sample letters and lessons that clarify expectations and encourage interesting, sincere, and lively writing: www.loc.gov/loc/cfbook/letters/.

Once students have written and submitted letters for this contest, it is also exciting for them to send the letters to the authors who are still alive. This is a simple matter of making an extra copy and sending it to the author in care of the publisher address on the copyright page of the book.

This is an effective way to get students to reflect on books that have made a difference in their lives, give them the opportunity to revisit these old friends, and express their feelings about them in letters that will actually be sent and read. Many students are excited by the idea of writing to authors of books they loved as young children, as well as to authors of books they have read recently. Therefore, announce your plans in advance to give students time to get copies of the books they want to discuss so that they can refresh their memories.

Of course, the final decision on whether to actually send the letter to the author or enter the contest should be left up to the student. This is another form of allowing young writers all-important ownership of their writing.

DAY 1:
Learning From Models: Content, Style, and Structure Techniques

Purpose
Students will:
- Identify elements of style and content in exemplar letters to authors
- Use strategies and techniques of exemplar letters in personal letters
- Write and revise a letter to an author

Materials
- Selected books students have read and enjoyed (from the library or supplied by students)
- Overhead and class set of exemplary letters written to authors (Sample Letter to an Author on page 75 and other models, from your own collection or from the Letters About Literature contest Web site)
- Overhead and class set of Techniques in Letters to Authors (page 74)
- Optional: Overhead and class set of Letters About Literature criteria and entry coupon. (*Note*: Because criteria and deadline may change from one year to the next, you should download this from the Web site each year. The submission deadline is usually the first week in December.)

Instructional Suggestions

1. Introduce the assignment and set a date for students to bring in the book they will write about.

2. On the assigned day, bring in a book that's been popular with students and model ways for them to refresh their memories about their books. Show them where to locate key names (e.g., front and back jacket, inside flap, first few pages), how to skim for important passages, and where the publisher's address is located on the copyright page, in case some students decide to send their letters to the authors as well as the contest.

3. Hand out Techniques in Letters to Authors and display it on the overhead. Discuss the techniques with your students.

4. Tell students that before they write their letters, they will read some sample letters for ideas on how to format the letter and develop its content.

> ## Techniques in Letters to Authors
>
> An effective letter to an author should . . .
> - Create an **attention-getting introduction** and include the **name of the book**
> - **Explain** how the book **changed your view of the world** or of yourself
> - Address the author; remember, you're not writing for the teacher
> - Provide explanations or **examples, anecdotes,** and/or other **specific details** to support your reaction to the book
> - Not summarize the plot or analyze literary elements—the author knows the plot
> - Not discuss the author's techniques, unless he or she uses a technique that draws you into the story in a personal way, such as the way Mark Haddon wrote *The Curious Incident of the Dog in the Night-Time* from the perspective of the autistic boy to help the readers understand what goes on in the mind of an autistic person and to see the world through his eyes
> - **Correspond** with the author as if you were having a discussion with him or her
> - Use **language** that is natural, clear, and specific
> - Write a **conclusion** with closure, that is, a final sentence that says in a few words something about the author's overall effect on you

5. Distribute copies of sample letters to read and use as models. Project a sample on the board and read it aloud. Go through each of the techniques for an effective letter and have students identify where in the sample the writer used each technique. Underline and annotate key words and phrases so that students see the techniques in use; you'll find a sample annotated letter on page 69.

6. Assign the students to work in pairs on one letter for each pair, annotating in the same way.

7. When pairs have finished their annotating, go around the room and ask each pair to read out loud the sentence that fulfills each category. For example, first ask pairs to share introductory sentences with grabbers. The class will then hear a variety of grabber openings. Then ask them to read sentences that explain how the book changed a student's view of the world or self, and the class will hear a variety of ways that writers can do that.

8. Invite students to add to the list of techniques if they have noticed others that have not yet been suggested. These might be:
   - Describe a character who has affected you
   - Explain why you feel a particular scene is important
   - Mention other books you have read by the author
   - Thank the author for writing the book

9. Have students make a web or brainstorm a list of ways the book they are going to write about changed their view of the world or themselves, evidence of how they changed, and events in the book that support this.

10. Assign students to review the sample letters again, noting that the organization of ideas is unique for each

Below is a sample of annotations on a student's letter to Louis Sachar.

Dear Louis Sachar,

    I've been thinking about some of my favorite books, and I thought of *Holes*, your story about a boy who gets prosecuted for a crime he didn't commit. He is betrayed and sent to the harshest and hottest climate that you can think of. He tries to make friends with the other boys sent there because the boys have to work as a team to make it through the day alive.

Introduction

    <u>Before I read *Holes* I didn't like to read.</u> I had no motivation or passion for it. I thought reading was boring and a waste of time. <u>After reading *Holes* I took on a whole different attitude about reading. If kids pick the right book to read, it is one of the most fun things to do.</u> If they are forced to read a book for school it could be boring and they won't like it. I remember when I <u>was reading *Holes*, I got sucked into the book and felt like I was right alongside Stanley</u> in Camp Green Lake being constantly dehydrated and exhausted and smelly. I still love to read chapter after chapter about Stanley on his adventure. You painted such a great picture in <u>my mind of Stanley and Zero in an underground boat, living off of preserved peaches and onions. I still laugh when I think of Mr. Sir with a face the size of a melon.</u>

Attention getter

How the book changed me

Example

    Holes taught me another lesson. Before I read *Holes* I spent a lot of my time playing video games and watching T.V. Now I know not to waste all of my time sitting in front of a screen and not spending enough time outside with my friends in the fresh air and sunshine. <u>Stanley is constantly outside, and he learns to like it and to work with his friends. Now I get my friends outside to do things like play ball and hike in woods.</u>

Natural, specific language

Conclusion

    <u>*Holes* also taught me that no matter how bad the conditions are, when there are friends to help, and there is teamwork, you can get through most anything. Thank you, Mr. Sachar, for getting me outside and for helping me to actually enjoy reading.</u>

Closure

                     Sincerely,

                     Erik Perry

letter and that there is no set formula in the order of the paragraph topics, except for the introduction and conclusion, because the letters flow in the order of each writer's personal experience with the book.

11. For homework, students should write at least half of their letter. Our directions are at right.

Homework

Complete the draft of your letter to an author. Try to write at least 150 words as a start. Remember, if you submit your letter to the contest, it must contain the minimum number of words required for your grade level by the contest.

DAY 2:
Using Revision Strategies and Editing Skills on Sample Letters

Purpose

Students will:

- Use standard letter format
- Understand letter-to-the-author techniques
- Apply appropriate revision strategies from One-Sentence Stories to the letter

Materials

- Overhead and class set of Draft Letter to an Author (page 76)
- Students' drafts of their letters to an author

Instructional Suggestions

1. Tell students that before they begin reviewing the drafts of their letters to an author, they are going to practice revising someone else's letter. "Whose?" they may ask, hoping it will be that of someone they know. But you can assure them it's by "Anonny Mous." They'll figure that one out.

2. Hand out copies of Draft Letter to an Author and ask students to take out their copies of Techniques in Letters to Authors. Read the first paragraph aloud:

   I had to do a book report for school, so I read *The Watsons Go to Birmingham—1963*.

   Ask what Casey, the author, got right in this first paragraph. (He named the book and he told something about himself, although not much, only that he had to do a book report.) What's missing? (An attention-getting introduction, what some people call a "grabber." Nothing "grabs" the reader with this sentence—and there is no suggestion of something about him that might be changed because of reading this book, which is why he's writing to the author in the first place.) Ask for suggestions from the class for adding to the introduction. A revised introduction might look something like this:

   "You gotta read this book," my friend told me. Yeah, sure, I thought. I don't much like to read, but I needed something for a book report. So I read what my friend liked, *The Watsons Go to Birmingham—1963*.

   Point out that this revision has a "grabber" by beginning with the bit of dialogue, tells more about the writer, and has a more conversational tone.

3. Ask students, working in pairs if you wish, to work through Casey's draft, identifying evidence of the techniques, indicating what's missing, and suggesting what needs to be added to the letter. Call students' attention particularly to the requirement that they explain how the book changed their lives and provide specific examples, anecdotes, and/or details, not just a plot summary.

4. As students analyze and revise Casey's letter, use the overhead or PowerPoint to identify particular places in the letter that need attention. If students need some direction, give it to them; this exercise is to prepare them to be critical readers of their letters so they can recognize areas needing revision.

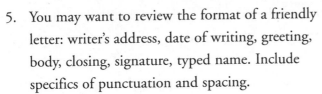

5. You may want to review the format of a friendly letter: writer's address, date of writing, greeting, body, closing, signature, typed name. Include specifics of punctuation and spacing.

6. For homework, ask students to revise their drafts. Our directions are at right.

Homework

Review your drafts, keeping in mind what you learned by revising Casey's letter. Also consult your Personal Record of Strategies and Skills. Then make the necessary revisions in your letter to the author.

DAY 3:
Using Revision Strategies on Students' Own Author Letters

Purpose

Students will:

- Revise their drafts for clarity of purpose, appropriateness of details, and logic of development and of conclusion

Materials

- Students' drafts of their letters
- Students' copies of Techniques in Letters to Authors
- Overhead transparency of Draft Letter to an Author (page 76)
- Overhead transparency of Revised Letter to an Author (page 77)

Instructional Suggestions

1. Begin by examining Casey's first draft. Display it on the overhead and ask a student to read the first paragraph aloud. Now ask students what they noticed about the opener, briefly reviewing yesterday's discussion of effective grabbers.

2. Have another student read the second paragraph and again ask students what they notice, having them consult their notes and revisions from the previous day. Guide them to discuss the choppy sentences and lack of fluency, highlighting how the idea in one sentence doesn't seem related to the next. Remind students of the workshop on writing one-sentence stories to create fluent sentences. Review the following:

   - participial phrases
   - prepositional phrases
   - infinitive phrases
   - dependent clauses

   Now display and read aloud the revised second paragraph. The idea of the brothers (now we know their names, Kenny and Byron) putting each other down and Kenny's laughing at Byron's getting his tongue stuck on the car door mirror because he was kissing his reflection now seem logical—related. Casey added some information about the family in a prepositional phrase (*about a family and two brothers*) and a dependent clause (*who were always trying to put each other down*).

3. Ask another student to read paragraph three of the draft version and ask students what they notice about the writing. Help students see the choppy sentences and unnecessary repetition. Now look at the revised version and point out how the writer revised: He added more important details from the story and his personal responses to those events. Also, most of these details are presented in prepositional and infinitive phrases and dependent clauses that improve the fluency of the paragraph and eliminate the unnecessary repetition.

4. Work through the next two paragraphs in a similar fashion, pointing out how the revision fleshes out the original draft with relevant details from the book that affected the student writer and changed his life (in this case, his awareness of the sometimes tragic consequences of prejudice). These details, essential to the assignment, are expressed in dependent clauses and modifying phrases attached, of course, to independent clauses. These are ways for writers to revise their drafts to add necessary and engaging details and, in the process, eliminate the choppiness and distracting repetition.

5. Give students time now to review the drafts of their papers, deciding how to improve fluency and add relevant details to explain how the book they read has changed them in some way. Don't rush this process. If they complete their revisions in class, ask them to annotate their letters as they did Erik Perry's letter to Louis Sachar. Otherwise, they can do the annotation at home.

6. For homework, assign a date for students to bring in their revised, final letters for peer response in Writing Circle. Our directions appear at right.

> ## Homework
>
> Revise your papers based on what we did in class today. Bring *all* drafts of your writing, including today's annotated draft, placing the most recent on top. We will be exchanging drafts for peer response during our next meeting.

DAY 4:
Peer Response in Writing Circle

Purpose
Students will:

- Recognize the techniques of an effective letter as applied in a student letter
- Follow Writing Circle procedures
- Complete the Writing Circle Peer Response form

Materials

- Overhead and class set of Writing Circle Peer Response to Letter to an Author (page 78)

Instructional Suggestions
This stage of the writing process is described fully on pages 37–39; here is a brief outline of the steps.

1. Remind students that they will be responding as readers and writers in ways that will really help one another. Tell them again:

When a writer receives a response sheet that has lots of comments and quotes, it feels great. Do this for your classmates and be sure to honor their writing efforts with thoughtful and specific responses to the questions on the response sheets that show you read and appreciated their writing.

6. Distribute Writing Circle Peer Response to Letter to an Author (one copy to each student). Put it on the overhead projector and read it over with the class, answering questions and clarifying terms.

7. Collect the students' letters and redistribute them so that no student has his or her own letter. Tell the students to read the letter and complete the response thoughtfully.

8. Allow time to return the letter with responses so the authors can read the attached responses from peers. Assign students to make revisions and edits tonight based on suggestions from their peers and ideas they had today; they will submit their letters with all drafts and peer responses attached to the teacher for Teacher Edit. You might use the rest of the class lesson time to allow students to read one another's letters or address envelopes to their authors, or to fill out the contest entry form.

Techniques in Letters to Authors

An effective letter to an author should . . .

- Create an **attention-getting introduction** and include the **name of the book**

- **Explain** how the book **changed your view of the world** or of yourself

- Address the author; remember, you're not writing for the teacher

- Provide explanations or **examples**, **anecdotes**, and/or other **specific details** to support your reaction to the book

- Not summarize the plot or analyze literary elements—the author knows the plot

- Not discuss the author's techniques, unless he or she uses a technique that draws you into the story in a personal way, such as the way Mark Haddon wrote *The Curious Incident of the Dog in the Night-Time* from the perspective of the autistic boy to help the readers understand what goes on in the mind of an autistic person and to see the world through his eyes

- **Correspond** with the author as if you were having a discussion with him or her

- Use **language** that is natural, clear, and specific

- Write a **conclusion** with closure, that is, a final sentence that says in a few words something about the author's overall effect on you

Revision Lessons You'll Love to Teach © 2008 by Ruth Townsend Story and Cathleen F. Greenwood, Scholastic Professional.

Sample Letter to an Author

Dear Louis Sachar,

I've been thinking about some of my favorite books, and I thought of *Holes*, your story about a boy who gets prosecuted for a crime he didn't commit. He is betrayed and sent to the harshest and hottest climate that you can think of. He tries to make friends with the other boys sent there because the boys have to work as a team to make it through the day alive.

Before I read *Holes* I didn't like to read. I had no motivation or passion for it. I thought reading was boring and a waste of time. After reading *Holes* I took on a whole different attitude about reading. If kids pick the right book to read, it is one of the most fun things to do. If they are forced to read a book for school it could boring and they won't like it. I remember when I was reading *Holes*, I got sucked into the book and felt like I was right alongside Stanley in Camp Green Lake being constantly dehydrated and exhausted and smelly. I still love to read chapter after chapter about Stanley on his adventure. You painted such a great picture in my mind of Stanley and Zero in an underground boat, living off of preserved peaches and onions. I still laugh when I think of Mr. Sir with a face the size of a melon. *Holes* taught me another lesson. Before I read *Holes* I spent a lot of my time playing video games and watching T.V. Now I know not to waste all of my time sitting in front of a screen and not spending enough time outside with my friends in the fresh air and sunshine. Stanley is constantly outside, and he learns to like it and to work with his friends. Now I get my friends outside to do things like play ball and hike in woods.

Holes also taught me that no matter how bad the conditions are, when there are friends to help, and there is teamwork, you can get through most anything. Thank you, Mr. Sachar, for getting me outside and for helping me to actually enjoy reading.

Sincerely,

Erik Perry

Draft Letter to an Author

Directions: Review the following letter to see if the writer has included all the elements of an effective letter to an author. If he has, underline and identify them; if he hasn't, indicate what is missing and suggest what the writer could do to include these elements.

Dear Christopher Paul Curtis,

I had to do a book report for school, so I read *The Watsons Go to Birmingham—1963*.

At first I thought it was a really funny book. These two brothers were always trying to put each other down. One of the guys got his lips stuck on the car door mirror and the other guy thought that was funny. He helped him anyway.

Then the family goes to Birmingham. While they were there four little girls got killed in a church. They were killed because they were black. This part of the book is true.

Kenny was really upset and had a bad time. He hid out behind the sofa and didn't want to fight with his brother anymore.

This book made me understand how bad prejudice is. Your book showed me that people of color are just like everyone else on the inside.

Sincerely,

Casey Kelly

Revised Letter to an Author

Dear Christopher Paul Curtis,

"You gotta read this book," my friend told me. Yeah, sure, I thought. I don't much like to read, but I needed something for a book report. So I read what my friend liked, *The Watsons Go to Birmingham—1963.*

At first I thought it was a really funny story about a family and two brothers who were always trying to put each other down. I had to laugh out loud when Kenny described Byron getting his lips stuck on the frozen car door mirror because he was kissing his reflection.

Then the family went to Birmingham to visit relatives. That's where something terrible happened that changed Kenny's life and mine. I couldn't believe that four little girls were murdered in a Sunday School at church just because they were black. I cried right along with Kenny because I knew those were real children who were killed. This really happened in Birmingham, Alabama, in 1963.

Kenny was so upset he couldn't get over the murder of children about the same age as he was, which is the same age I am. Even after the family came home, Kenny crawled behind the sofa and stayed there most of the time. He didn't want to eat, he didn't even want to tease Byron. Kenny told the story in his words the way he saw it and felt it. This made me feel like I was right there with him crying for those little girls. This also made me understand that prejudice against black people or any people different from you can lead to murder.

Reading your book showed me that people of color or people different from me on the outside are really the same as everyone else on the inside. Thank you, Mr. Curtis, for helping me learn a lot about other people and about myself.

Sincerely,
Casey Kelly

P.S. I thanked my friend for telling me about *The Watsons Go to Birmingham—1963.*

Writing Circle Peer Response to Letter to an Author

Student writer: _____ Date: _____

Responder: _____ Book title and author: _____

Task: Responder should read the letter. On the dotted lines, copy words or phrases from the letter that fulfill each of the elements listed in the space provided.

1. Copy a phrase from the letter that explains how a book changed the student's view of the world or self.

   _____

   _____

2. Copy two phrases that give explanations or examples, anecdotes, and/or other specific details to support the letter writer's point of view.

   _____

   _____

3. Copy a phrase with which the letter writer relates the book to him- or herself rather than asking the author questions about why he or she wrote the book.

   _____

   _____

4. Copy a phrase that tells the author how the student reacted when reading the book.

   _____

   _____

5. Copy a word or phrase that stood out to you or was the strongest.

   _____

   _____

UNIT 4:
Writing for Understanding

Professional writers, when asked by novices for advice on how to write successfully, always say, "Write about what you know." One thing we teachers know is that our students do their best writing when they write about themselves—what they think, believe, experience. Our task is to build on their eagerness to share what they know by creating writing assignments that will engage them personally in expository formats for real audiences.

Decoder List of Revision Strategies

- Focus on a topic
- Relevance
- Logical conclusion
- Fluency—sentence structure
- Imagery—word choice
- Imagery—tone
- 3-D characterization
- 3-D characters—dialogue

Revision Exercise and Writing: Photos Alive

"Writers are like photographers," you tell your students.

"Oh, yeah—how's that?" they ask.

"They do what you do as a writer—they focus on a subject, a person or group, a place or thing or event, and they try to capture a feeling or mood," you say. "And they tell a visual story that people looking at the photograph will pick up on."

"That's cool, so let's take pictures instead of write stories," they suggest.

"Not so fast," you say, "because you as a writer can tell the stories hidden beyond the obvious and take the readers into a fully alive world. You use language to create what you might call verbal snapshots that can do what the photographer can only suggest in a photograph. You can give your snapshots flesh and bones, pulsing blood, and lively speech. With language you can create sensory images that give dimension and animation to a photograph."

You may go on to explain that photographers, like writers, learn to focus on their subjects and to look beyond the obvious for the stories waiting to be told, either in visual or in verbal images. Photographers can only suggest those stories in their medium, but with language, writers can make those hidden stories come fully alive. Writers can enable readers to feel the silky softness of a newborn kitten's fur; savor the fragrance of freshly baked pizza and the bittersweetness of rich dark chocolate; sway to the rhythms of Dixieland; and cringe at the sight of starving animals left homeless in the wake of Hurricane Katrina. All of these sensory experiences give dimension and life to writing, but writers have to know how to use the tools of their trade to make it happen.

With that explanation, you're ready to help your students bring photos to life.

DAY 1:
Learning to Read a Photograph and Make It Come Alive With Words

Purpose
Students will:
- "Read" a photograph
- Focus on one element of the photo (one person or group)

- Write and revise a brief description of the image that incorporates dialogue and appeals to the senses

Materials

- Photographs of people (students can bring in photos of family, friends, or ancestors, or you may provide images from collections, such as *A Day in the Life of America* [Smolan & Cohen, 1986])
- Evocative photographs by outstanding photographers such as Annie Leibovitz, Alfred Eisenstaedt, Margaret Bourke-White, Dorothea Lange, Matthew Brady, and Steve McCurry (many of these photographers' images are available on the Internet)
- Overhead transparency or PowerPoint slide of one photograph to use for demonstration purposes
- Draft and revised versions of story about your selected demonstration photograph (draft may be written in class, but the revised version should be prepared beforehand; see Day 2, Step 3)

Instructional Suggestions

1. Ask students to look closely at the photos they brought to class or selected from the collection. Assure them that each photo has a story in it about a significant event in someone's life. Psychoanalyst Robert Akeret (2000) says:

   "Out of photos, long and fascinating stories begin. There are three stories for every photograph: the story we find depicted in the photograph, the story behind it, and the story we project onto it. Perhaps it is where these three stories intersect that we find the 'true' story we have been searching for."

   Explain that they will follow some specific steps to read a photograph, a process that requires curiosity and imagination, qualities all of them have in abundance. Model the process for students by using your demonstration photo; here's an example Ruth uses with her students.

   - Put your photo on the overhead or PowerPoint projector. For example, one I've used that works well is of an old man with a boy about 9 or 10 years old, each bundled in heavy winter clothing, standing beside a large horse-drawn sled (called a pung). The old man stands erect and looks solemnly into the camera, but the boy, head titled to the side, leans slightly toward the man.
   - I tell students I'm interested in the relationship between the boy and the man, who is the grandfather.
   - The winter scene in this old black-and-white photo could be cold and bleak, but I see warm affection for the grandfather in the boy's eyes and stance.
   - The two figures are about to use the sled. I imagine the scene, where they are going, and what they are saying to each other.
   - In my little story—a verbal snapshot, really, of the photo—I want to reveal something about the two people and their relationship.

2. Now invite students to read their own photos by following the prompts below. Have students jot down their responses to the questions as they study their photos, giving them adequate time to write.
   - Look at the photo and get a first impression, reading it from left to right, then up and down.
   - Ask yourself: What do I feel right now? What moves me most about the photograph?
   - Is there anything about it that disturbs me?

- Come up with a descriptive word or phrase that captures the whole feeling behind the photo.
- Study each person in the photograph individually. What one or two words come to mind to describe each one?
- Insert yourself into one pictured person's skin, asking yourself, "What is she or he feeling?"
- Look at the photograph for clues to relationships between people. Are they touching, and, if so, how? Are they making eye contact with one another? What messages might be passing between them?
- Imagine that these individuals could move and talk. How would they move? What would they say to each other?
- Go over the photo several times, trying to pick up something you may have missed that suggests a personality and/or a relationship.
- Imagine the story that might be behind the image. How did the people get to this point? What are they going to do next? Why are they posed the way they are? What does the image represent about a person or relationship?

3. Now students are ready to draft the story they see reflected in the photo. Remind them that their goal is to make the stories behind the photos come alive. Give your students some time, maybe 15 to 20 minutes, to complete their drafts. We encourage you to write your own draft along with them, deliberately leaving out dialogue and sensory details. Or you may display a first draft you've written outside of class.

DAY 2:
Using Revision Strategies on Sample and Student Photo Alive Stories

Purpose
Students will:
- Review and revise their story drafts, adding dialogue and sensory details

Materials
- Student story drafts
- Overhead of draft and revised versions of story about your selected demonstration photograph

Instructional Suggestions
1. Put your draft on the overhead for students to read. Here is the sample we share that goes with the photo described in Day 1, Step 1:

Gramp called me to get on the pung, a kind of big wooden sled. I asked him where we were going and he said to the sap house to make maple syrup. I asked him all kinds of questions about the process, but he didn't talk much. As we bumped along the snow-covered road to the sap house, I could see the horse's breath in the cold air. I wanted to help make the syrup, so Gramp let me help him build the fire in the grate where he boiled the sap. I learned a lot that day about making maple syrup.

2. Ask your students if the description makes the people in the photo come alive. Guide students to notice what's missing; for the sample above, that might be:

- a sense of the relationship between Gramp and the boy
- evidence of the personality of each character
- sensory appeal
- dialogue

3. Show students your revised vignette, the one you prepared before class. Ask students to compare it to the draft. Here's a revision to the sample above.

"Hop on," Gramp calls to me from the pung, a kind of big wooden sled. I climb up next to him and ask, "Where are we going?"

"I have to start the fire and begin cookin' down the sap."

"How long will it take?" I ask.

"A good part of the mornin', I expect."

"Can I help?" I ask.

"Maybe."

Gramp doesn't talk a lot, at least not to me. I asked him once, "Why don't you talk more?"

"Talkin' keeps you from workin', and I got lots of work to do."

We keep bumping along to the sap house as the horses, their steamy breath like frosty vapor in frigid morning air, pull the pung through the snow-covered old road.

When we get to the sap house Gramp says, "Bring the firewood down and lay it alongside the trench."

As I pick logs from the pile stacked along the wall, Gramp crumples pages from a Montgomery Ward catalog and puts kindling on top. Then he adds logs and lights the fire. After the crackling flames die down a little he spreads pans out on the grates and fills them with sap. We stand and watch for a long time until the sap begins to bubble.

"How much sap does it take to make syrup?" I ask.

"Somewheres between 36 to 40 gallons of sap for one gallon of syrup."

"How long does it take to make it all?"

"Most of a month if the weather is right."

"What's right?" I ask.

"Freezin' nights and warmin' days keep the sap flowin'," he says.

A few days later Gramp says, "Let's go check the syrup."

The aroma of maple syrup in the sap house is so strong I feel like I'm tasting it. Gramp takes a ladle and scoops up some of the light brown stuff from one of the big pans.

"David, use that spoon over there and take a little bit of syrup to taste. Don't burn your tongue."

Carefully I fill the spoon with the hot syrup, wait for it to cool to warm, and put the spoon to my lips and suck in the gooey liquid.

"What do you think?" Gramp asks.

"Well, I kinda like it. But I guess it just needs pancakes and butter."

4. Ask your students what makes the photo come alive in the revised version. For our sample, responses include:

- Dialogue: adds sounds to the action and reveals something about the personalities of the boy and his grandfather, such as the boy's eagerness to be with his grandfather and to please him; or the grandfather's taciturnity but also his understanding of the boy and his fondness for him
- Sensory appeals: the smell and taste of the syrup, the feel of the cold and the heat of the fire and boiling syrup, the vision of the old man and the boy and of the horses pulling the pung along the snow-covered road, the preparation of the fire and the grate, and the sampling of the syrup
- Use of first person and present tense to pull the reader into the action and give an immediacy to an event from long ago

5. The next step is for students to work in pairs or small groups to review their story drafts to decide ways for them to add appeals to the senses, including dialogue, to make their photographs come alive. Encourage students to share their revised stories along with the photos that inspired them with their classmates; they can also be displayed in the classroom and/or in the school library. You may even decide to create a bound anthology called "Photos Alive!"

Writing a Personal Essay and Using Revision Strategies

In many classrooms the most frequently assigned writing is the expository essay because it is the form most frequently required in standardized testing. For that reason, the essay is often considered formulaic, arcane, and boring—nothing you would ever write for a real audience. However, the truth is that essays are popular with all kinds of audiences on all kinds of subjects. And it is true that the essay follows a general pattern just as many poems and stories do, but that makes them easier to write and to read. It also gives writers freedom to write about any subject, even themselves, with the assurance that real audiences appreciate an engaging, well-written essay.

More good news is that there are many places for students to send this kind of writing, and so this assignment can be offered to your young writers with authentic audiences and purposes in mind right from the beginning; see page 14 for a list of contests and publications that seek young writers. In addition, personal essays can be submitted along with school and college applications—another motivation to revise with care.

DAY 1:
Reading Models of Personal Essays

Purpose
Students will:

- Identify elements of style, literary techniques, and content in exemplar personal essays

Materials

- Overhead transparency and class set of "Leap of Faith" (page 87) and a few exemplary personal essays written by students (pages 87–90 or from your own collection)

Instructional Suggestions

1. Tell the students they will be writing a personal essay, but first the class will read some sample essays for ideas on how develop their writing for content and style.

2. Distribute copies of sample essays to read and use as models. Project Sample 1 ("Leap of Faith") on the screen or SMART Board and read it aloud.

3. Ask students to identify the features they notice in the essay, such as:

   - **First-person narrator**
   - **A "grabber" beginning or lead** (that the writer is atop a telephone pole)
   - **Focused subject statement or thesis** (what the writer wants to explain about her experience)
   - **Examples or details to develop the thesis** (in this case, the challenge of the climb, including the writer's internal conflict)
   - **Conclusion** that reveals something about the author or something she gained from her experience (in this case, that she could overcome her fear and gain confidence in herself)

4. Ask students to point out these features and label them on the sample. Point out that not all personal essays, even though they are written in first person, need to focus on the writer. Writers can write in their own voice about something or someone they have observed. The personal part of the essay is when writers convey the meaning or insight or understanding gained from their observation. (See Sample 3 "The Cotton Club.")

5. Have students read samples 2 and 3 and generate a list of essay features with their partners, annotating the phrases in the essays that reveal those traits. When they have had enough time, have the pairs share their findings, which should include something like the list on Techniques You Can Use in a Personal Essay (page 91).

DAY 2:
Planning a Personal Essay

Purpose

Students will:

- Draft a personal essay
- Apply revision strategies practiced in Photos Alive to include imagery, varied sentence structure, and 3-D characterization

Materials

- Student notes from Photos Alive
- Overhead transparency of Techniques You Can Use in a Personal Essay (page 91)
- Optional: Overhead transparency or slide of photo from Edward Steichen's *The Family of Man*
- Class set of Planning the Personal Essay (page 92)
- Overhead transparency of Attention-Getting Leads (optional: a class set of the handout on page 93)

Instructional Suggestions

1. Return the notes and photos from Photos Alive to your students. Remind them that the photos represent a story about a personal experience or a human condition that led them to a realization or sudden insight into a universal human truth.

2. Tell students that they are going to flesh out their vignettes from Photos Alive into personal essays. This format offers more room to express the realization or awareness about life that the story behind the photo hints at.

3. Distribute copies of Techniques You Can Use in a Personal Essay and compare with student notes from yesterday's exercise. Encourage students to share ideas for transforming their verbal snapshots into personal essays using the techniques discussed. For those students whose essays are based on their own experiences as suggested by the photos, you might want to refer them to the student samples. And for those students whose essays are based on photos that depict a universal human condition, you might have your students examine selections from Edward Steichen's book *The Family of Man*. A particularly evocative black-and-white photo from the Dust Bowl days of the 1930s is of a young mother with her children.

   • Walk your students through the reading of this photo (see pages 80–81 of Photos Alive)
   • Invite them to select another photo from Steichen's book or the materials recommended in Photos Alive

4. Now hand out the Planning the Personal Essay sheet. Allow students time to fill out their planners, offering help where needed. Ask them to star five or more techniques from the handout that they plan to use in their essays, and start adding these features to the essay planners.

5. If your students ask you about the "required" number of paragraphs, direct them to look again at the sample essays. There is no magic number. This might be a teachable moment about paragraphing—when to begin a new one, especially with dialogue, and what goes into a paragraph, sometimes only one word, sometimes a hundred or more.

> ### Resources on Teaching the Personal Essay
>
> Refer to books in the Scholastic Professional Series such as *Nonfiction Writing: From the Inside Out* by Laura Robb, or *Teaching Powerful Writing* by Bob Sizoo, or any other good books on composition for help if you need it.

6. When the planning is done, turn students' attention to writing engaging leads. Distribute the handout Attention-Getting Leads. Read through and discuss the different types of leads and how they work. Have students write at least two different leads in class; they can choose which one works best for their essay.

7. Assign students the task of completing the essay as homework, citing the due date as a day for peer response in Writing Circle. Encourage them to create a title for their essay, using the strategies learned in the Headline News lesson. Suggest that they might find the title in a word or phrase from the essay.

DAY 3:
Peer Response in a Writing Circle

Purpose

Students will:

- Respond to one another's' writing in nonjudgmental ways that help the writers
- Share their writing with readers
- Consider their readers' comments
- Make notes on final edits and revisions

Materials

- Overhead and two copies per student of Writing Circle Peer Response to a Personal Essay (page 94)

Instructional Suggestions

On Writing Circle day, remind students that they will be responding as readers and writers and in ways that will really help one another. Tell them again: "When a writer receives a response sheet that has lots of comments and quotes, he or she feels important. Just the way you like to feel. Do this for your classmates and be sure to honor their writing efforts with thoughtful and specific responses to the questions on the response sheets that show you read and appreciated their writing."

This stage of the writing process is described fully on pages 37–39; here is a brief outline of the steps.

1. Distribute two copies of the Writing Circle Peer Response to a Personal Essay to each student. Put a copy on the overhead or PowerPoint and read it over with the class, answering questions and clarifying terms.

2. Collect the students' essays and redistribute them so that no student has his or her own. Tell the students to complete the forms thoughtfully.

3. Allow time to return the essays so the authors can read the attached responses from peers. Assign students to:
   - Make revisions and edits tonight based on suggestions from their peers and ideas they had today
   - Print one copy of the final revised and edited essay and staple it on top of today's draft and responses to submit in class on the assigned date

   On the assigned date, students submit their final essays with all drafts and peer responses attached for the Teacher Edit.

Samples of Personal Essays by Students

Sample 1
Leap of Faith
by Missy Walker, grade 7
Scholastic Writing Award: National Silver Medal, Regional Gold Key Award

Never, not once in my life, have I ever thought that I would find myself standing atop a telephone pole. It's not a thought most people have, and not something most people have experienced. So, the majority of humans can't really imagine what it feels like. But I don't have to imagine. I know.

How did I find myself standing some thirty-five feet up in the air on top of this pole, you may be wondering. And *why* was I up there in that incredibly dangerous situation? Well, first of all, it wasn't dangerous. I had a harness on, to catch me when I jumped.

I was up there because I was trying to push my comfort zone; we all were. To get to the top we had to climb up using these staples in the pole as foot and hand holds. I remember standing up on them, one at a time, all the while wondering why everyone had been so scared. It was just like going up the stairs, I thought. But when I reached the top, I realized why everyone had been so freaked out.

I tried to stand up, but slipped. I caught myself, luckily, and tried again. Wobbly, like a newborn foal, I stood on top of the pole. It was shaking beneath me, or was that my legs? Accidentally, I looked down, and suddenly realized why everyone had been so petrified. It was like everyone had checked their fears at the top of the pole, and then jumped, leaving behind a great big heaping pile of anxiety for the next person. *Why am I up here?!? I have no harness!!!* I tricked myself into thinking, *If I jump, I'll smash into a million pieces because there's nothing there to catch me!* But then, in the midst of my state of panic, I looked down at all the people that had gone before me, and saw that they were all in one piece, safe and sound, making me realize that I *did* have a harness on and I'd be totally safe when I jumped.

"GO!" somebody suddenly yelled. I, like everyone else, ditched my fears on the top, and like a well trained dog, jumped on command, unthinkingly, unknowingly, just feeling myself falling through the air, feeling like I was flying on invisible wings. That is, until the harness rope abruptly caught me, snapping me back to life. I was lowered to the ground, my legs still wobbling from those terrifying moments at the top. People rushed to ask me, with looks of excited nervousness on their faces, saying, "How was it?" I glanced up at the top, still slightly petrified, saying with false ease and a relaxed air, "No problem."

Sample 2
Magic
By Jesse Wayne, grade 8
Scholastic Writing Award: Regional Gold Key Award

"President!" Andrew screamed enthusiastically. He had only been playing for two rounds and he was already beating everyone else. We were all between fourteen and sixteen. Andrew was eight.

"Come on, Andrew!" Austin shouted, "I needed *one* more turn!" We had been living on the boat,

Integrity, for about a week now. We were a group of fifteen friends (seven parents and eight kids), not including the crew and guides. When we weren't snorkeling, eating, drinking, hot tubbing, jumping off the top of the boat, watching *Smallville*, or walking on the islands of the Galapagos, we were playing Presidents, an incredibly addictive card game.

"Guys, let's go." Klaus, our rather good looking Ecuadorian guide, summoned us down to the boarding deck to get on the pangas, small, inflatable boats used to transport us from boat to island. We had all been sitting around in our wetsuits drinking hot chocolate and playing Presidents for about ten minutes, waiting for the adults to get dressed.

"Let's," said Johnny. We all stood up and stretched. Face and Andrew ran down the stairs, swung across the metal pole that stood supporting the staircase, and leaped into the pangas. Their mother began to scold them for running on the boat and called them to put suntan lotion on. Whining their protests, they obeyed. The rest of us stepped into the pangas.

The first panga filled up with kids and set off for the snorkeling destination on the new island with Klaus as our guide. It was another magical day in the Galapagos.

We circled the island slowly, the pearly white beaches glinting in the sun. There were small brown dots barking in the sand: sea lions. Above us, a pelican circled and dove into the water. Two seconds later, he reappeared on the surface with a crab squirming in his beak. To our left was an island of stone, strewn with awkward, skinny pink figures that bobbed and squawked at us as we sped by. If this wasn't paradise, what was?

We slowed as we neared a cave in the boulder wall of a cliff, about fifty feet high. "Okay guys, you know the routine; don't go in the cave because of the currents and try not to touch anything. Over we go." He plunged backwards into the water. I washed the shampoo out of my goggles (to keep them from fogging) and did the same.

Icy cold water surged into my wetsuit and down my snorkel. Around me, seven other figures splashed into the water. I spit the water out of the snorkel and began swimming.

I was swimming in a rainbow, thousands of fish swimming around me, curious to see what I was. I stuck out my finger and one nibbled at it. I looked down to see Klaus break his own rule; he reached his hand out and pulled a mussel off the rock. Breaking it open, he began to feed the fish. Fish the size of my eyelash and the size of my leg crowded around him, trying to get a snap at the tasty treat. A fish the size of my finger stole the mussel out of his hand, only to then be eaten by a bigger fish. Klaus handed me a broken mussel and I began feeding the fish. Hundreds of fish swarmed around my outstretched hand, pulling and biting at the morsel. I took a deep breath and dove down into the crowd fish. All of a sudden, they were gone.

I looked up to see what had caused this disturbance and saw two shadows swimming around the surface of the water. They swam closer and closer, sleek and graceful. Two small fins protruded from their backs. One circled me and the other swam underneath my feet, sending a slimy feeling up through my leg. All of a sudden, a face, much like a dog's, popped up two inches from my own and stared me straight in the eye. "Hello, Mr. Sea Lion," I thought to myself. It darted away, trying to provoke me to chase it. I swam after it obediently.

They were two female adolescents, playful and curious. They often dove off the rocks to play when they saw a panga full of people approaching. They were just children looking for playmates. We had to be cautious. If an anxious mother or protective male were nearby, it could mean bad news.

I streaked after the sea lion. She slowed and let me come a foot close to her sleek coat, and then spun and dashed underneath my toes. I spun after her and grazed her tail with my finger. The sea lion hurried away and then stopped and looked at me. Sea lions are intelligent, enough so to play tag, and now the sea lion was It. I began swimming, weaving, spinning, whatever I could do to avoid the sea lion. But, nothing could trick this master of the waters. Wherever I swam, she swam, wherever I wove, she wove. Soon enough she swam right over me and gently touched my arm with her head.

Nearby, the other sea lion was playing with the others. Klaus had pulled out a handkerchief and was waving it around in the water. The sea lion watched it, intrigued by the foreign object. It flashed its teeth and grabbed the handkerchief, all within a millisecond. A tug-of-war had begun. Klaus and the sea lion dueled for what seemed like hours. Finally, with a mighty tug from both ends, the handkerchief split in two.

Ironically enough, this was considered an average morning in the Galapagos, but then again, the Galapagos aren't exactly average. Every day was unique and special; I played and indirectly communicated with sea lions, I danced with a mighty albatross who was looking for a companion, was spit on by an angry marine iguana, and experienced possibly the most untouched and beautiful sunset there is to see on this earth. I can truthfully say that magic really does exist. You only have to know where to find it.

Sample 3

The Cotton Club

by Eugene Stockton-Juarez, grade 9

in *The Best Teen Writing of 2007: Selections From the Scholastic Art and Writing Awards*

I jerked up suddenly from my sleep as the car gracelessly went over yet another pothole on 116th Street.

Resigned, I looked out the window to my side. Before me lay the incoherent sprawl of Harlem—the usual broken-down brick buildings, the shattered glass, the boarded-up storefronts. Once the jewel of the New York art scene, Harlem had finally and obviously succumbed to middle-class flight. My father, ever the nostalgic poet, had dragged me out here once again to wax sentimental over the days of Langston Hughes. One only had to turn one's head, I thought to myself, to see that there was nothing left here. The passion and the beauty were gone, given over to the pulsing hordes of the desperate.

The usual crack smokers huddled along the sidewalks, right out in the open. One or two leered at me with blackened teeth. A little girl sat with them, huddled up in a blanket against the wall. I *guessed* it was a girl—she had long hair that blew in the cold wind. I averted my eyes and fiddled with the radio. At a stop sign a woman made a few tentative steps toward us. Dad waved her on, looking at me surreptitiously, clearly hoping I hadn't noticed. I pretended I hadn't.

We had no particular place to go that night. Dad just wanted to drive past the shells of buildings that might themselves recall some lingering note of Duke Ellington, some enduring word of Ralph Ellison.

The car crunched to a stop in front of the sad remains of the original Cotton Club. I stepped out onto the street, pulling my jacket tight around me. Dad's shoulders were slumped as he stood mesmerized by the wall of graffiti. It was too bad, I thought, that this was all there was left for him to look at.

I looked around at this travesty of society. Unlike my father, I didn't see the pain of reality, but rather the pointless expression of what wasn't. Perhaps that is the only defense of those who witness such things in the early 21st century. It is said that we only see what we wish, so maybe it is also true that what we wish not to see we absorb as a lesser reality, less deserving of our concern. In any case, what I felt, though I am ashamed of it, was not pity but boredom.

I wandered around a bit as Dad held his hand up to the cold brick. I looked down toward Spanish Harlem, then back up the street. There just wasn't anything to focus on. Then a shifting movement to my left caught my eye: a blind beggar sitting on a street corner. At least he seemed blind. He didn't focus on anything I could see. He scraped his jingly soda can across the sidewalk and smiled. As the occasional person went by, the beggar never changed his oddly contented appearance. I pulled a dime out of my pocket and dropped it in the can. He kept on smiling. I dug around and found a quarter, dropped that in, too.

A group of businessmen turned the corner onto 116th Street. Seeing the three of us—Dad with his hand on the wall, me loitering on the curb, the smiling beggar on the pavement—they closed ranks, avoided eye contact, pulled their long coats around them. As they passed, it struck me that the scene had become mystifying and almost poetic—a beggar surrounded by the billowing black cloaks of rich white businessmen. The men each glanced at the beggar and then walked on, at a quickened pace. They scurried in that puzzling way we humans use to run from the rain even when there is no shelter in sight—as if to comfort ourselves from the face of the inevitable, from the fact that we are indeed running.

I watched the businessmen recede toward downtown. I could hear their conversation start up again, loud and opinionated. Looking back to the smiling beggar, I noticed that he'd managed to get to his feet. He glanced at me once, barely meeting my eye from under his knit cap, then shuffled off slowly. The wind blew. Leaves and trash gathered in the spot where he had sat. I watched him go. Dad was saying something, but the wind blew it away.

The beggar hobbled past the crack smokers, now sitting on a stoop. He stopped in front of the child, still huddled in her blanket, but obviously awake now, playing with some scrap of something. He dropped the can in her lap. She looked up. And then he just kept walking, evenly, slowly, probably with that same smile, until he turned the corner and I couldn't see him anymore.

As we worked our way through the snarling traffic of Manhattan, it occurred to me that I had just witnessed something profound. I try not to think about it too much, not to read too much into it. But it's a nice memory. It takes the edge of an otherwise blank and disappointing evening. It makes it not quite so awful that Langston Hughes is dead and that Duke Ellington doesn't play at the Cotton Club anymore.

Techniques You Can Use in a Personal Essay

(quotes from student sample "Leap of Faith" by Missy Walker)

1. First-person narrator

   (*Never, not once in my life, have I ever thought that I would find myself standing atop a telephone pole.*)

2. Subject statement

   (*And why was I up there [atop a 35-foot telephone pole] in that incredibly dangerous situation?*)

3. Thesis (what the writer will explain or explore)

   (*I was up there because I was trying to push my comfort zone.*)

4. Details (that explain or develop the thesis)

   (*I tried to stand up, but slipped. I caught myself, luckily, and tried again. Wobbly, like a newborn foal, I stood on top of the pole. It was shaking beneath me, or was that my legs?*)

5. Narrator learns something or gains some insight

   (*But then, in the midst of my state of panic, I looked down at all the people that had gone before me, and saw that they were all in one piece, safe and sound, making me realize that I* did *have a harness on and I'd be totally safe when I jumped.*)

6. Attitude/tone of the narrator can be serious or funny or sad, or all three

   (*I glanced up at the top, still slightly petrified, saying with false ease and a relaxed air, "No problem."*)

7. Vivid word choice

   (*I, like everyone else, ditched my fears on the top, and like a well trained dog, jumped on command, unthinkingly, unknowingly, just feeling myself falling through the air, feeling like I was flying on invisible wings.*)

8. Imagery

   (*To get to the top we had to climb up using these staples in the pole as foot and hand holds. I remember standing up on them, one at a time, all the while wondering why everyone had been so scared. It was just like going up the stairs, I thought.*)

9. Dialogue (sometimes internal dialogue)

   (*Why am I up here?!? I have no harness….If I jump, I'll smash into a million pieces because there's nothing there to catch me!*)

10. Varied sentence structures

    (*It was just like going up the stairs, I thought. But when I reached the top, I realized why everyone had been so freaked out.*)

Planning the Personal Essay

The grabber or lead paragraph:

Focused subject statement:

Examples or details to develop the subject:

Conclusion that reveals insight or understanding:

Attention-Getting Leads

Task: Read the different narrative leads below, used by award-winning student writers to start their own personal essays. Try writing a few different narrative leads of your own, experimenting with different styles (Action, Dialogue, Essayist's Thoughts, Setting the Scene). Then choose the narrative lead that works best for your piece.

1. **Action:**

   I was so excited I nearly took the door off its hinges! I ran out quickly and guided my bike to the garage. My father yanked off the training wheels with a tool, and put them on the shelf in the garage. We went up our steep hill, onto the street. ("Goodbye, Training Wheels" by Amber Kinui)

2. **Dialogue:**

   "President!" Andrew screamed enthusiastically. He had only been playing for two rounds and he was already beating everyone else. We were all between fourteen and sixteen. Andrew was eight.

   "Come on, Andrew!" Austin shouted, "I needed one more turn!" We had been living on the boat, Integrity, *for about a week now. We were a group of fifteen friends (seven parents and eight kids), not including the crew and guides . . . playing Presidents, an incredibly addictive card game.* ("Magic" by Jesse Wayne)

3. **Essayist's Thoughts:**

   I've come to the conclusion that the Mattei family cannot do anything nor can they go anywhere without causing mayhem or havoc of some kind or another. Let's start at the beginning of what a normal day to me would be. ("My Family Extravaganza" by Sandy Mattei)

4. **Setting the Scene:**

   As we approached the gaping hole that writhed down into the ground and into the night, I could feel the anticipation and nerves that circulated through our group like an electrical wave. I shivered at the sudden awareness of tumbling emotions that encircled us. ("The Shadow, The Drip, and I" by Anna Carroll)

Writing Circle Peer Response to a Personal Essay

Student writer: _____ Essay title: _____

Peer responder: _____ Date: _____

Student writer's request to responder: Ask a question about something you would like to learn from your responder. _____

_____

Peer responder:

1. Reply to the student writer's request as written above.

    _____

    _____

2. Copy a phrase or a sentence that describes the subject of the essay.

    _____

    _____

3. Copy a phrase or sentence that offers the thesis—what the essay will describe or explore.

    _____

    _____

4. Copy two different words or phrases that offer details that explain or develop the thesis.

    _____

    _____

5. Copy a phrase or sentence that offers vivid word choice and/or imagery.

    _____

    _____

6. In your own words, write a sentence that describes the insight the narrator gained from the experience, or the lesson learned.

    _____

    _____

7. Suggest where this essay should go public (circle): *Teen Ink*, Scholastic contest; *Writing* magazine; *High School Writer*, school newspaper/literary magazine; other: _____

8. Add a positive comment or compliment. _____

Unit 5:
Writing for Literary Expression

Storytelling is a natural part of the human condition. We all love to tell stories and hear stories regardless of our age. So naturally, our students want to write stories, especially short ones. And we want to build on their enthusiasm for the genre, but we also know that it's a demanding task and that guiding our students through the process takes longer than one or two days; we need to plan the learning activities over several days.

Story writing is a demanding writing genre, and certainly justifies the most attention to revision. To engage our students in this process and keep them excited about their writing we begin the unit with a playful revising exercise that also addresses essential revision strategies as well as the basic elements of story. Have fun with it and the story writing.

> **Decoder List of Strategies**
>
> - Imagery—word choice
> - Imagery—tone
> - 3-D characterization
> - 3-D characters—dialogue

Revision Exercise and Writing: Chicken of the Week*

This exercise invites students to write and revise character profiles. Although students will be doing the hard work of revising for concise, vivid language and lively characterization, watch for some smiles as they write and eagerly share their humorous characterizations of . . . chickens!

DAY 1:
Reading and Writing Character Profiles

Purpose

Students will:

- Create characterizations in a few words
- Show, not tell
- Describe a character's appearance, what the character does and says, what others say about him or her, and how others react to him or her
- Develop a vocabulary of descriptive words
- Set a tone

Materials

- Photos of chickens and a rooster or two
- Sample of cartoon birds (such as Tweety Bird, Chicken Little, Babs and Ginger from *Chicken Run*, or other birds that are cleverly anthropomorphized)

*Lesson idea inspired by Pete and Gerry's Organics Egg, 140 Buffum Road, Monroe, NH 03771. You can visit Pete and Gerry's Web site at http://www.peteandgerrys.com/.

- Samples of brief but engagingly written characterizations (see pages 97 and 98 for models)

Instructional Suggestions

1. Tell the class that they have a very important job to do; they must capture the personality of a chicken in writing. You may get some funny looks, and that's okay. Explain that at Pete and Gerry's Organic Eggs in New Hampshire, the owners use the farm's star chickens to advertise their organic eggs in local newspapers and on their egg cartons. The farmers welcome help with the advertising campaign, so tell your students they are going to help Pete and Gerry by creating some mini-bios for the chickens.

2. Show transparencies or PowerPoint pictures of cartoon chickens and other animals such as Tweety Bird, Babs and Ginger (from *Chicken Run*), Snoopy, Garfield, Morris, and so on. Ask your students what they all have in common. Typical responses we've received include the following.

   They all:
   - Have distinct human-like personalities
   - Talk, at least in bubble form
   - Interact on a human level
   - Do human things
   - Display human emotions

3. Show transparency or PowerPoint photographs of real chickens and ask your students what they notice. Images are available from online sources such as Y! Chickens (many color photos and cartoons) and Chicken Wikipedia (many color photos and interesting scientific, historical, and literary information). You may also ask students to do a Web search on chickens. Finally, ask students what they notice about these feathered creatures. Our students generally respond with comments such as:
   - Chicks are cute.
   - They all look pretty much alike.
   - There's not much evidence of personality.

   "Terrific," we say. "That gives you a clean slate to give some chickens personalities—the more distinctive or outrageous, the better."

4. Distribute a brief scientific description (use the Internet—search for "chicken") of the chicken and the rooster, in part to give students something basic to work from and to acquire some basic vocabulary. Don't belabor this; just ask your students to look it over and refer to it if needed when they begin their writing.

5. Next, explain the assignment. We might say,

   > Imagine that an egg farmer wants to advertise his product in a clever way to get your attention. And suppose you come up with the idea to have your chickens talk about themselves and their eggs. After all, it's the chickens who produce the eggs, right?

   "Right," students agree—maybe reluctantly, because after all it's chickens we're talking about. So now explain that each student is going to sponsor a chicken and invent a name and a personality for her and write about her in a mini-bio. (It's okay if some students want to choose a rooster, as long as they understand that roosters don't lay eggs.)

Revision Lessons You'll Love to Teach

6. Now model the process of brainstorming ideas about a chicken and drafting a mini-bio:

    - Put a photo of a chicken on the screen.
    - Give the chicken a name and briefly describe her. I tell my students that I've named my chicken Belle because I've also decided that she's from Alabama, so she's going to be one of those stereotypical "Southern belles."
    - Display your first draft, which should be lacking in detail. You may use the one I've written about Belle:

    Version 1
    Belle
    Belle is a beautiful chicken from Alabama. She won the Dixie Chick contest.
    She says she likes to lay eggs and that they are the cutest eggs in the henhouse.

7. Ask students if this bio reveals much about Belle's personality or creates a picture of her. Obviously this is not an engaging snapshot of Belle—nothing you'd want to read. But why not? Student may note that the bio:

    - Doesn't reveal much about her personality, except maybe that she's proud of her eggs
    - Doesn't have Belle say or do anything that shows what kind of "chicken" nature she has
    - Tells about Belle but doesn't show us Belle

8. Next, display a revised version of the chicken biography; a new one for Belle is below:

    Version 2
    Belle, the Dixie Chick
    You can't miss Belle; she insists on roosting in the sunniest, warmest nest in the henhouse.
    "Well, of course, honey, Ah'm from Alabama," she clucks and bats her big, brown chicken
    eyes just like Scarlett O'Hara. "Did you know I won the Dixie Chick contest because I lay
    the cutest little ole eggs in the henhouse? And they taste just as wonderful as they look.
    Cluck, cluck, bruuuuck, y'all!"

    Ask students what the writer does to show the personality of Belle. They may point out:

    - What she does: roosts in the warmest nest, bats her eyes like Scarlett O'Hara, the quintessential coquette
    - What she looks like: big, brown flirty eyes
    - What she says: won the Dixie Chick contest, lays cutest, best-tasting eggs in the henhouse
    - That Belle has a Southern accent as in *Ah'm little ole Belle, y'all*
    - That it gives a picture of a Southern belle, an exaggerated picture
    - That it's "like a funny cartoon character" (Yes! you say; that's the idea)
    - That it creates a humorous tone by comparing a chicken to Scarlett O'Hara and having her win the Dixie Chick contest

9. At this point you may want your students to begin writing their Chicken of the Week bios; if so, skip to step 14. But if you think they need another example, you might use Adelaide's mini-bio.

Version 1

Sweet Adelaide

All the chickens in the henhouse like Adelaide because she is nice to everyone. She isn't pushy at feeding time and she doesn't do any henpecking because she wants all the chickens to be happy so that they'll lay good eggs.

10. Ask students if this version reveals much about Adelaide's personality and creates a picture of her. They may say that:

   • It doesn't reveal much about her personality, except she's nice (whatever that means) to the others
   • She doesn't say or do much of anything to show her "chicken" nature
   • Like the first version about Belle, this bio of Adelaide doesn't show us Adelaide

Then show them the revised bio of Adelaide.

Version 2

Sweet Adelaide

Ask any chicken in the henhouse about Adelaide, and you'll hear that she is the sweetest, most even-tempered chicken in the henhouse. She never nudges others out of the way at feeding time, and she never would even think of henpecking another chicken. "Certainly not," she says, smiling sweetly. "I see only positive qualities in others. We're all in the same business of laying eggs, so I want us all to feel good about ourselves and be happy. Everybody knows that happy chickens lay better-tasting eggs. Bruck, bruck . . . . bruucrock."

11. After you've displayed the revised version, ask students what the writer does to show the personality of Adelaide. They may note:

   • What she does: never pushes or shoves others at feeding time; never pecks at other hens
   • What she looks like: she smiles sweetly
   • What she says: sees only positive qualities in others; wants everyone to feel good about themselves and be happy so they can lay better-tasting eggs
   • That it gives a picture of Adelaide

12. Point out to your students that the revised versions of Belle and Adelaide avoid using the following over-used, nonspecific words because these words don't show us a picture:

   • good   • wonderful   • bad   • terrible   • big
   • great   • nice   • sad   • mean   • pretty
   • ugly   • awful

13. Encourage students to find more specific words and phrases to show what they mean by *awful* or *bad* or *great* or *wonderful*.

14. To get your students started on creating their Chicken of the Week bios, suggest this list of notable chickens and invite your students to add to the list:

   • Edith, the no-nonsense businesswoman
   • Tammy, the Valley Girl

- Marilyn, the movie star
- Edna, the henhouse dorm mother

If you need some roosters:

- Red, the cowboy
- Burt, the gangster
- Clarence, the nearsighted geek
- Chuck, the handsome dude

15. You may want to offer a couple of fill-in-the-blanks opening sentences on the board:

    (chicken's name), the (character description in a phrase) of the henhouse, is Pete and Gerry's Chicken of the Week. (chicken's name) loves to (action of the chicken that reveals her characteristic).

16. Encourage students to continue their chicken profiles, using all of the tools and strategies of characterization. You might wish to project these on the board as they appear in the Decoder List.

17. Remind the students to go back into their writing to revise for vivid word choice. Consider projecting the Decoder List definition of this strategy on the board.

18. Give students time to take out their Personal Records. They should review the skills and strategies they have copied to apply revision strategies they have needed in past writing.

19. Have fun with these mini-bios while emphasizing the characteristics of writing that show rather than tell and therefore create characters the reader can envision in three-dimensional color. Add photos of chickens to the revised mini-bios and hang a different one in your classroom each week—and send the best ones to Pete and Gerry.

Writing a Short Story and Using Revision Strategies

This series of lessons helps students put the revision strategies introduced in the Chicken of the Week activities to work on their own original short short stories. Be sure to remind your students that their finished stories can be submitted to magazines and contests for young writers, pointing out the lists and postings on your Places to Go Public bulletin board. This kind of real audience motivation is especially important for a writing project as comprehensive and demanding as writing a story.

DAY 1:
Brainstorming Story Ideas

The first big hurdle involves helping our students brainstorm some story ideas. We tell them that all writers, regardless of the kinds of stories they write, always begin with what they know. Although they may fictionalize people and events from their lives, change the settings, and alter the endings, the basic stories they tell are rooted in real life. Even J. K. Rowling draws from what she knows of actual boys and girls, teachers and parents, and bad guys and good guys to create the Harry Potter stories. Therefore, we're going to begin the story-writing process by brainstorming for ideas from our lives, as all authors do.

Purpose

Students will:

- Draw story ideas from personal experiences and events in their lives
- Use graphic clustering to brainstorm for details

Materials

- Overhead transparency or chart paper, on which you'll model clustering story ideas
- Overhead transparency of Nathan's Cluster for "Granddad's Glove" (page 101)

Instructional Suggestions

Take the heat off your students and help them to brainstorm by beginning a list of what writer Lou Willett Stanek (1996) calls "trigger words and phrases" from your students' lives that will stimulate their memories of people and events that have story potential.

1. Write "Trigger Words and Phrases" on the chalkboard or SMART board. Explain that everyone has words and phrases that conjure up people, events, places, and all kinds of experiences, each of which has a story connected with it just waiting to be told.

2. Model brainstorming a list of trigger words and phrases, pausing briefly to describe the story each reminds you of. For example, we might begin by walking our students through the process Nathan went through; he is the author of "Granddad's Glove" (pages 113–115). Nathan let his mind wander freely through his world—his interests, activities, experiences, concerns (see above box), knowing that any one of these words could generate a story.

3. Invite students to brainstorm their own lists of trigger words.

4. Once you sense that each student has collected a substantial list of words and phrases, ask each of them to select one word or phrase that has particular meaning for him or her—that has a story in it. For example, Nathan selected *baseball* from his list because his granddad told him about playing baseball when he was a kid and wanting a baseball glove.

5. Demonstrate the prewriting process by displaying Nathan's cluster of story details (p. 101). Nathan was impressed with what his grandfather had told him about his childhood, and he needed to record all the details his grandfather had shared on paper. Nathan used a process called clustering (sometimes also called webbing). Point out how Nathan put his trigger phrase, *Baseball with Granddad*, in a circle and branched off from the central idea. On each branch, he wrote a detail related to his grandfather's memories of baseball, such as names of people, places, incidents, conflicts, feelings, and so on. Your students will see that as a writer thinks of one detail, others come to mind. As they do, writers should capture them. Encourage students to write everything down, and model filling the board with clusters of details related to a trigger word of your own.

> **Nathan's Trigger Words and Phrases**
>
> shopping at the mall
> McDonald's
> soccer
> *Dancing with the Stars*
> iPods
> blogs
> summer camp
> 9/11
> cell phone
> "awesome"
> 7-Eleven
> Wal-Mart
> Britney Spears
> *Ugly Betty*
> baseball
> global warming
> "Bye, Bye, Miss American Pie"

6. Now let students work on their own clusters. Walk around the room, encourage their thinking, and ask some leading questions of those who seem stuck. When you sense that students have run out of steam, put them in pairs to share their clusters. Encourage each student to ask his/her partner any questions that a cluster detail generates, such as:

- Why was that important?
- What happened then?
- Who saw you do that?
- How did you feel about that?
- When did you go there/do that?
- Where was this place/what did this place look like?

This discussion process will further help students flesh out details that they may use in their stories. Besides, it's fun. Our students like to talk about themselves and their experiences.

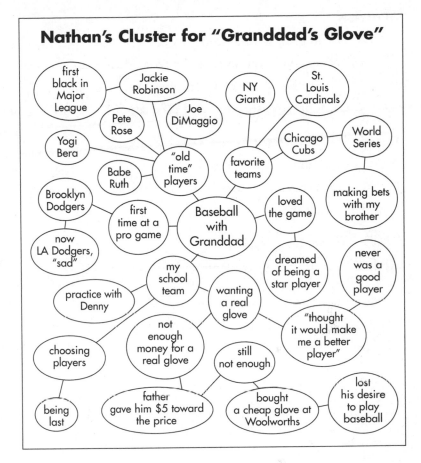

Nathan's Cluster for "Granddad's Glove"

7. Collect the clusters and review what students have written, looking to see if they have details that can be the basis for a story, complete with characters, a plot with conflict and resolution possibilities, a setting, and an opportunity to show something about the human condition. You will be reviewing story elements in the next lesson; we find it helpful to highlight and name the possible story elements we see on each student's cluster and ask some questions to generate more details where they seem to be needed. (Caution: These clusters are *not* to be graded.) Be sure to return these clusters to your students at the next class session.

DAY 2:
Drafting the Story

At this point your students are still enthusiastic about their own experiences. We want to build on that enthusiasm, but we also want them to recognize the elements and techniques of a story so that they can model the development of their own stories on those of other writers.

Purpose

Students will:

- Recognize story elements from sample stories
- Plot a storyboard
- Draft a story

Materials

- Handout of sample student stories (pages 110–115)
- Transparency and class set of Basic Story Elements handout (page 106)
- Class sets of Character Planning Sheet, Setting Planning Sheet, and Plot Storyboard (pages 107–109)
- Optional: transparency and class set of brainstorming cluster "Granddad's Glove" (page 101)

Instructional Suggestions

After you return the brainstorming clusters to students and before you ask them to begin their story drafts, review with them one or two short short stories written by other students. This will give your students some confidence that they too can create an interesting story and it will give you an opportunity to help them recognize the basic elements in the story.

1. Distribute sample stories "Tip Tap" and "Moving Forward." Point out that these stories were written by students just like them—and they won awards! Give them time to read the stories and make some initial comments as to what they liked or admired in each story (no negatives allowed). They are likely to comment on the description of the characters and the dialogue, especially since they have already worked on creating character descriptions in Chicken of the Week. You also hope they'll say something about the storylines, that is, the development of the plot from beginning to resolution.

2. At this point your students are ready to review basic story elements. Distribute the handout and discuss. Don't belabor it because it will be a review for them, but ask them to keep it handy in their notebooks as a reminder of the essential elements of their short stories.

3. Walk your students through one of the two sample stories, identifying these elements from the Basic Story Elements handout:

   - The main character (**protagonist**) and the secondary characters
   - The incident (**inciting event**) that stirs the protagonist in some way to response or action
   - Actions/events in the **rising action**
   - The **turning point** that determines the outcome of the story
   - The **setting** and its significance
   - The final **resolution** of the plot
   - The **purpose** of the story

4. Distribute the Character and Setting Planning Sheets and invite students to think through their stories by working on the sheets. You may want to model this process with your own story if your students need support.

5. Have students look at their story clusters and character and setting planning sheets. Distribute the Plot Storyboard and have them plot their stories. As they work on their storyboards, encourage them to add to their clusters but also to delete what now doesn't seem relevant to the story they want to create.

6. You may want to walk your students through the process of selecting details from their clusters. If so, display and discuss the brainstorming cluster for "Granddad's Glove" (page 101). You may say,

   Nathan wants to focus on the story his grandfather told him about wanting to buy a baseball glove many years ago when he was in fifth grade. Initially he wrote in the cluster everything he thought of that Granddad told him. Now Nathan has to select the appropriate details from his cluster as determined by the story elements and put them in his Plot Storyboard. As he begins to do this, Nathan may realize that he needs some more information from his grandfather. If he can get it, fine. If not, he can invent it. And this is an important point: Neither Nathan nor any of you needs to write a "true" story (unless you choose to). The "real" incident or person may be, and most often is, just a springboard for the storyteller. So inventing characteristics to reveal a personality or inventing details to develop a conflict, arrive at a resolution, and reveal some insight into human nature (the story's purpose) is what storytelling is all about.

7. We tell our students that if they need to confer with one another, that's fine, because that's what most writers do: get feedback from one another.

8. For homework they can complete their storyboards, if need be, and draft their stories.

DAY 3:
Revising I

Now the real writing begins. As students begin to revisit their first drafts, we need to give them all the help we can by drawing on the revising strategies and language skills we've been using in other real writing assignments and by calling on some famous writers to help us. Who wouldn't appreciate having Charles Dickens or Sandra Cisneros or Ray Bradbury or Jane Yolen as mentors for our students? Always learn from the best, we say.

Purpose

Students will:

- Recognize and use story techniques employed by mentor writers
- Apply writing and revising strategies practiced in Chicken of the Week and Headline News
- Revise their short story rough drafts

Materials

- Transparency and class set of Sample Mentor Texts (pages 116–117)
- Basic Story Elements handout (students have copies in their notebooks)

Instructional Suggestions

1. Explain that the first draft of a story is mostly a time to get the basic elements in place. Now it's time to get to the real business of crafting a short short story. That means creating an engaging "grabber" beginning that will pull readers right into the action by introducing the characters and at least suggesting the conflict and, in some cases, the setting.

2. To give them some ideas, share sample story openers from selected authors. Distribute copies of Sample Mentor Texts. Give students time to read them, or read them aloud.

   Note: It's important to offer students a variety of sample opening paragraphs—at least five. If you offer only one or two samples, you run the risk of having every story opening sound alike. As we advise in the next step, give students time to read the excerpts in class and a chance to discuss or describe the techniques.

3. Ask students what they notice about each opener; jot techniques on the board as they are identified so

that students will have a list of possibilities for their own opening paragraphs. Their responses might include the following kinds of observations:

One writer, Sandra Cisneros, seems to tell her own story—she writes in first person. You might want to explain that doesn't mean it's necessarily her story, only that the writers assumed the persona of the storyteller, as did Mark Twain when he wrote *The Adventures of Huckleberry Finn,* and James Berry (Sample 4), whose story is told by a young girl.

Most of the writers write in third person; they keep a distance from the story. Here's a chance to point out that Nathan may tell the story of his grandfather's efforts to get a baseball glove from a third-person perspective. Or he could write in first person, assuming the persona of his Granddad the way James Berry wrote his story in the persona of a young girl. Writers can tell their stories from any point of view they choose—as long as they are consistent in that point of view.

Ray Bradbury's story begins with dialogue, and then we find out it has been raining for seven years! Yes, and something is going to happen, but we don't know what. Bradbury has grabbed us and made us want to find out what is about to happen and where in the world—or beyond— it would rain constantly for seven years!

Stephen Crane sets a scary scene of men on a tiny boat in the ocean. He grabs us. We want to know who these men are, how they got there, and what's going to happen to them. O. Henry does much the same thing: He pulls us right into the conflict Della is wrestling with—not having enough money, despite her efforts, to buy a Christmas present. We want to know what is so important about the present, what she's going to do, and how the conflict will be resolved.

Jane Yolen begins her story like a fairy tale. And it's going to be about a couple's frustrated desire for a child. We want to know what's going to happen and if this fairy tale will have a happy ending, because not all do.

Dickens just says, "Marley was dead, to begin with." A blunt statement, and then he shows us a man named Scrooge—the name itself unpleasant, even ominous—who obviously took charge of "anything he chose to put his hand to."

4. Give students time to review their story beginnings and revise them to engage the reader as one of the mentor writers does. Encourage them to confer with one another as they write and revise.

5. Review the revision strategies introduced in the

> **Tip**
>
> Of course, you may select your own story openers, particularly those from works your students have already read and enjoyed. And you want to make available to students the short stories from which the Sample Mentor Texts came. Assign your students to select and read at least one of these stories to study the ways the mentor writers create believable characters and settings, develop logical plots, and reveal insight into human nature.

Chicken of the Week lessons:

    Imagery—word choice

    Imagery—tone

    3-D characterization

    3-D characters—dialogue

    In addition, remind students to check their Personal Record of Strategies and Skills for revision techniques that might benefit their work.

6. For homework, ask students to continue reviewing their first drafts, focusing on characterization, setting, and plot development, and to bring a revised draft of their story to class on the day assigned. (Try to assign this homework over a weekend so students have more time to spend on it.)

DAY 4:
Revising II

Purpose

Students will:

- Respond to peers' stories as critical and positive readers
- Complete Writing Circle Peer Response to a Short Story form

Materials

- Two copies per student of the Writing Circle Peer Response to a Short Story form (page 118)

Instructional Suggestions

On Writing Circle day, remind students that they will be responding as readers and writers in ways that will really help one another. Tell them again: "When a writer receives a response sheet that has lots of comments and quotes, he or she feels important. Just the way you like to feel. Do this for your classmates and be sure to honor their writing efforts with thoughtful and specific responses to the questions on the response sheets that show you read and appreciated their writing."

This stage of the writing process is described fully on pages 37–39; here is a brief outline of the steps:

1. Distribute two copies of the Writing Circle Peer Response to a Short Story form to each student. Put a copy on the overhead or PowerPoint and read it over with the class, answering questions and clarifying terms.

2. Collect the students' stories and redistribute them so that no student has his or her own story. Tell the students to complete the forms thoughtfully.

3. Allow time to return the stories so the authors can read the attached responses from peers. Assign students to:

- Make revisions and edits tonight based on suggestions from their peers and ideas they had today
- Print one copy of the final revised and edited story and staple it on top of today's draft and responses to submit in class on the assigned date

5. On the assigned date, students submit their final stories with all drafts and peer responses attached for the Teacher Edit.

Basic Story Elements

When we begin to craft anything, from a fence or a wooden boat to a design for a poster or a short story, we need some tools and guidelines. As writers, our tools are words and our rich English language, and as story writers we also need some guidelines. Those are the basic elements of any kind of story.

Characters

- A story must have a **protagonist**, the person around whom the action centers or who drives the action.
- If a story has other characters in it, they must be important to the story, complicate the action, and either be in conflict with the protagonist or help the protagonist solve a problem or understand something. Other characters can also add color or humor to a story, but include them only if they have a relationship to the protagonist or affect the action in some way.

Plot

- To be a story, something has to happen. That action is the plot.
- A plot begins with an **inciting event** that stirs the protagonist in some way physically and/or emotionally to reach a goal, solve a problem, or come to an important understanding.
- In a short story, most of the rest of the plot, sometimes called **rising action**, focuses on the protagonist's efforts to reach his or her goal, whatever it is, until he or she reaches a turning point.
- The **turning point** in a story determines what the protagonist will do or what will happen to him or her; in other words, it determines the outcome of the story.
- The final part of the plot is its conclusion or **resolution**. You might even call it the result of the protagonist's journey/attempts/efforts to reach a goal.

Setting

- Every story happens in some context or **place** called the setting.
- Setting can be critical to a story; in fact, it can even be part of the inciting event (e.g., a hurricane or shipwreck).
- Setting creates the **mood** and atmosphere of a story.

Purpose

- Writers create stories to **make a point**. It may be to make the readers laugh or cry or be angry or enlightened or understand something or someone. A good writer doesn't tell his/her readers what the purpose of the story is; the writer shows it, pulls readers into the story so that they feel, smell, touch, taste, hear, and see what the characters in the story do.
- At the end of the story, readers can say, "Aha, now I get it" or "Yes, I understand why that happened, or how he felt, or why she did that."

 Revision Lessons You'll Love to Teach © 2008 by Ruth Townsend Story and Cathleen F. Greenwood, Scholastic Professional.

Character Planning Sheet

Task: Characters are the most important element in a story. It's what happens to them, whether they are humans, animals, bird, fish, robots, aliens, or even insects, that matters most to the reader. That means writers must create vivid characters, especially the protagonist (the main character), if they want their stories to be read. To help you imagine and develop your protagonist, answer the questions below.

Describe the age, gender, and physical characteristics of the protagonist:

_____

_____

Conflicts: Your protagonist must have some internal and external struggles, or **conflict**, to give your story a plot and to keep your reader interested. Of course, many external and internal conflicts are intertwined (e.g., a character wants to invite the unpopular kid to sit at the table, but is afraid the class bully might make fun of him for doing so), so don't worry too much about the labels for the conflict.

If you choose to write a story set in a historical period, such as during a war, conflicts might be built into your story for you. For example, your character might be a teen during World War II who is too young to enlist but lies about his age and joins the army anyway.

An **external conflict** might be an argument with a sibling, a parent, a bully, a coach, a friend, or an enemy platoon; or it could be a confrontation with a force of nature, such as a storm while sailing or ice while trying to get to class on time, or with a law or expectation in society, such as the draft during the Vietnam War or the age limit for a driver's license.

Describe possible external conflicts:

_____

_____

An **internal conflict** is a struggle within a character's heart or mind, such as whether to cheat on an exam, tell a white lie to make a friend feel better, or invite the unpopular kid to sit at the lunch table.

Describe possible internal conflicts:

_____

_____

Setting Planning Sheet

Task: Every story takes place somewhere. Sometimes the setting is significant to a story, in which case you need to focus more attention on the details of time and place. Other times, the setting is of minimal importance because the story could take place anywhere. Regardless of the significance of the setting, you need to make it come alive for your reader—and the more important the setting is, the more you focus on enabling the reader to see, smell, taste, touch, and hear what the character(s) in your story do because the setting, regardless of its role in the story, sets the mood. This means that you must select specific nouns, adjectives, adverbs, and verbs to pull your reader into the scene.

Identify the setting and scene of the story's action. Be specific as to place, time in history or year, season, or day.

_____

_____

Describe what you want the reader to see. Use specific language to show the relevant details of the setting (e.g., the wave-swept deck of the small sailboat as it cuts through the foaming surge of the waves).

_____

_____

Describe what you want the reader to smell. Be specific (e.g., the heavy odor of stale cigar smoke clinging to drapery in a humid room).

_____

_____

Describe what you want the reader to hear. Be specific (e.g., the steady squeak and swish of an ancient windmill lulling a child to sleep).

_____

_____

Describe what you want the reader to taste. Be specific (e.g., her tingling tongue as she savored the sweetness of the fresh-picked raspberries).

_____

_____

Describe the feel of something you want the reader to imagine touching. Be specific (e.g., the smooth silkiness of the kitten's fur; the painful cold of the freezing rain against his face).

_____

_____

Revision Lessons You'll Love to Teach © 2008 by Ruth Townsland Story and Cathleen F. Greenwood, Scholastic Professional.

Plot Storyboard

Task: Your story will need a beginning, middle, and an end. Read the definitions below for the parts of a story plot. Fill in your plans on the lines provided. Jot words or phrases in each category to give yourself the bare bones of your story. Fill in the plot events in any order you wish. For instance, you might want to describe the central climax or conflict first, then go back and fill in the exposition and rising action scenes.

Timeline

(Beginning) Exposition: Identify the protagonist and describe an opening event that gives a hint of conflict.

_____

_____

Rising action: List a few events or incidents that show the conflict(s) building and that move the story along.

_____

_____

Turning point: Describe an event that brings the protagonist's main conflict out in the open for the reader.

_____

_____

(End) Resolution: Describe an event or incident that wraps up the story and resolves the conflict in some way. (This does not have to be a happy ending, but it should show some kind of insight or recognition by the protagonist.)

_____

_____

Purpose: Explain what you think is the purpose or point of the story, what understanding, insight, or satisfaction you want readers to get from the story.

_____

_____

Short Short Story, Student Sample 1

Moving Forward

by Beth Tolmach, age 13

First Place, Short Story, Rippowam Cisqua School Writing Contest, Bedford, NY, 2006

The sky was a misty gray and a damp breeze ruffled Edna's honey blonde hair. She got out of her rusty car, slammed the door shut, and walked out onto the drab pavement. She was wearing her uniform, red and black shirt, black slacks, and tennis sneakers. Arriving at the glass doors of the Pizza Hut restaurant, she pushed the door and entered the dank aroma of cheap pizza and dull life. This was where she was trapped, for eight hours a day, serving chatty children or uptight adults inedible food. Her cheeks always hurt by the end of the day from all the fake smiling she put on, and she sported dark bags under her eyes.

Edna sighed, thinking about this, as she walked up behind the counter. She knew that this job was worth it. Maybe if she held the job for another year, she could attend college like some of her friends. She was two years out of high school already and proudly kept her diploma sitting on her bookshelf. In the evenings, when her feet were sore and her mind was exhausted, she looked at the diploma, which built up her determination somewhat.

Edna said a weak hello to other employees and sat on a creaky stool in the back. It was still morning, and customers weren't expected for a while. She bit on a cuticle, looked up at the clock, and fingered her charm bracelet. Things went slowly in Pizza Hut when all she had to look at was the crusty walls and the other strange workers. Her boss, Jerry, a hunched-over man who always seemed to squint, stood in the center of the room, darting his eyes around the room. He spotted Edna, who sat on the stool, and approached her.

"Edna, there's some kids out there for lunch. Can you take them?" he asked in his hushed tone. This was a surprise. It was only 11:30. Edna nodded glumly, and stepped from behind the counter, carrying the glossy menus. She almost forgot to bear her artificial smile, and her cheerful stride. She advanced towards the table, where a group of four or five teenage boys sat, throwing wads of paper at each other and laughing loudly.

"Hi guys," said Edna in her fake tone, "here are some menus. Would you like drinks or anything?"

The boys smirked.

"Uh," one said with a toothy grin, "what drinks do you have?"

Inside Edna's head, the wheels were turning, and she could see disaster looming.

"All types of soda, juice, milk, water," she listed, trying hard to stay cheery.

"Do you have any pineapple juice?" asked another boy, obviously thinking he was the wittiest person to ever have walked onto the face of earth.

"No," said Edna with gritted teeth, "We don't."

"What about mango juice?" said the boy, still ruthlessly smiling.

"Nope," growled Edna, starting to lose her patience.

"We'll all have Cokes then," sighed the boy, pretending to be in great agony.

Edna, soundlessly, turned sharply and proceeded to fill five glasses of Coca-Cola. She carried back the drinks on a platter, and put them one-by-one down on the table.

A boy dropped his fork on the floor.

"Uh, could I have a new one?" he asked.

"Sure," said Edna. She brought him a new fork. "Are you ready to order?" she chirped.

"Yeah," said one boy. "We're sharing a pizza with bacon bits and pineapple, and two garlic breads." Edna nodded. Then, the same boy who dropped his fork previously, let his fork fall to the ground again. Edna slowly looked down, and then back up at the boy.

"Can I have a new fork?" he asked innocently.

Edna gulped. She felt her anger building up, and her hands trembled. She picked up the fork, and clenched it. "No," she said. "You can't have a new one." She coolly walked away, and could hear the protest of the boys behind her.

Edna knew it was ridiculous that talking sharply to a bunch of teenage boys could make her heart beat with such excitement, but she couldn't help it. Edna gave the order to the food-preparers, and waited in the back, satisfied with her small achievement. She wouldn't be pushed around by people five years younger than she.

When the disgusting bacon pizza was heated and ready, she served it to the boys' table without a word. They were silent themselves, and gawked at Edna, as she served and then left. Edna felt the power of taking charge, and she liked it.

She waited in the back more, when Jerry came over to her, with a sour look upon his wrinkled face.

"Those boys over there've been telling me that you were rude to them," Jerry said, with curiosity in his voice. Edna froze. There was a long pause between the two of them, and then she shrugged. There was no use in lying. "They were being obnoxious towards me, so I told them off. What's wrong with that?"

Jerry looked at her with his cold brown eyes. For a moment he seemed sympathetic, but that quickly faded.

"There's nothing wrong with that," he said quietly. But then his voice rose. "When you're in the schoolyard! But you're not in the schoolyard, now, are you? This is a store, Edna! These are your customers! The customers are everything. Kids are kids, and just because these boys were being a bit annoying, is no reason for you to treat them that way!" Jerry's voice was sore, and worn-out, and Edna almost felt bad for starting this whole thing. Her empathy disappeared, when Jerry uttered those two painful words. "You're fired, Edna, I'm sorry. Between this, and your tardiness, I have no choice."

Edna looked down at her feet, and felt her eyes welling up with tears. She did her best to hold them in, and sniffled.

"I'm sorry, but it's what needs to be done. At the end of this day, return your uniform, and you can leave. I'll send you your last paycheck in the mail."

Edna said nothing. Her pride from five minutes ago was now being washed away with disbelief and sorrow. Her eyes were burning, and as soon as Jerry walked away, she let the hot tears spill out.

Edna flipped through the Help Wanted section of the newspaper. It was two weeks after her boot. She had gotten over it quickly. She realized a day later that she had despised the job. Perhaps her back talk to the teenagers was a good thing. Things were looking up; she was looking for a part-time job, and once she found one, would apply to colleges. Anything would be better than that putrid job serving old pizza to a rude bunch of kids. For the teenagers, Edna's response was just a tiny slice out of their boring lives. Things like that happened to the boys all the time. But for Edna, that moment was different. For her, she felt she was finally moving forward.

Short Short Story, Student Sample 11

Tip Tap

by Ryan Beiermeister, age 16

National Award Recipient, Scholastic Art and Writing Awards

OPEN! The neon light casts an orange glow that drapes across my nose.

It's not like I had big plans or anything. After high school I figured I'd take a break, pack up my Mustang, and drown my sorrows with the engine's purr. For the main course, I'd go to art school and get a nice job. But life has a way of smacking you in the jaw, doesn't it? Now I'm here. Mike's Mini-Mart. The midnight shift, with fluorescent lights attacking me from every angle. I'm starting to feel insecure about how my complexion is reacting. I look up at the mirrored ceiling, ignoring the disorderly aisles of junk, and examine my crumbling mascara. My appearance proves I've given up. As my boredom climbs, I strum my jagged fingernails along the plastic counter. The tiny black radio churns out "Songs of the Seventies" behind me. My head slumps down; I can feel my exhausted eyelids coming to a close. As I start to get fuzzy, I pray for a pleasant dream. Maybe a credit card, new car, or true love. Cling-clang-ring-ring! My momentary lapse from reality is interrupted by a cluster of bells. An ancient man with crinkled skin waddles in, his patent leather shoes slowly tapping against the linoleum floor. It's unusual to see the elderly at run-down convenience stores this late at night, especially men who can barely walk. I wonder what he wants.

That's the one perk of my job—it's interesting to see what people buy at midnight. Something desperately needed or desperately desired.

Regardless of my curiosity, I refuse to make eye contact. Exhaustion is pumping through my veins; I look like a train just hit me, and I'm a failure. Eye contact will surely bring this to his attention. The man slowly weaves in and out of the rows, making his way to the canned foods. I try to ignore him, but he is a label reader. With each massive ravioli or spinach can he reads, he clunks it down on the metal shelf, making me jump. His feet continue to tip-tap toward the refrigerators, stopping in front of the energy drink section. I would hate watching him read the labels of every energy drink, especially since the list of chemicals is endless, so I grab a magazine and turn my face to the cigarette wall. The glossy pages crinkle between my fingers as I read about the successful, rich, and happy. I almost vomit. Behind me I hear the suction lining of the fridge-door seal, and the taps get progressively closer. Our usual midnight customers make it quick—grabbing their beer, condoms, or Tylenol with Olympic speed. I swear the fluorescent light-bath scares them away.

Finally, I hear a soft thud against the plastic counter. A quick turn of my neck reveals the final purchasing decision. A pack of spearmint gum. A sting of annoyance hits me, but I decide to let it go.

"A dollar-nineteen please," my voice croaks out.

One-Two-Three-Four-Five-Six coins clink on the counter, followed by a crisp dollar bill. I appreciate the exact change. Section 6 of the Employee Contract requires me to always ask if they'd like a receipt. And always ask if they'd like a bag.

But tonight I'm feeling dangerous.

The man starts to tear open the pack of gum, and then places it in his palm. I turn my back, and listen to his slow tapping toward the door. As I let his image slip my mind, zoning back into a pathetic trance, I notice a sudden silence. His walking pattern abruptly stops. When I turn back around, the man is standing there facing me, looking at me as if I were a science specimen. After his peculiar head-to-toe examination, his bug-blue eyes zero in on my pupils.

"You may think it's rather late," he says, glancing at a gold wristwatch, "but we all deserve something more." Then he pops a piece of spearmint gum in his mouth and tip-taps out, the doorbells clanging behind him.

Short Short Story, Student Sample III

Granddad's Glove
by Nathan

Pleeeese don't pick me last, I pleaded under my breath, as the captains began choosing sides for a fifth grade softball game. I was a new kid in school, eager to play baseball and be on a team.

"You're on my team, Billy," Kenny said.

"I'll take George," Meylon said.

"I want Richard," Kenny said.

"Sherm, come on my team," said Meylon.

I noticed that the boys who got picked early had baseball gloves. The kids who were picked later, like me, didn't have them.

Before we started playing, Miss Burgis, our gym teacher, said, "There are eight boys with gloves. When your team is at bat please let the boys in the field use your gloves."

I was happy she said that. The softball was bigger than a baseball, but it didn't seem any softer when I tried to catch it with my bare hands.

Meylon's team was up first, so I got George's glove and went to the outfield. No balls were hit in my direction. In fact, not many balls were hit at all, and that allowed me to examine the glove I had. This was the first baseball glove I ever put on! It was a lot bigger than my hand and there was a big leather web between the thumb and forefinger. Also, the fingers were all held close to each other with a rawhide strip. There was a lot of padding over the thumb, the little finger and the base that covered the heel of my left hand, and that made a kind of "pocket" in the glove over my palm.

No balls were hit to me in the first inning, so I handed the glove back to George when we changed places. Someone hit the ball in my direction, and as I ran forward it bounced and hit me in the chest. I managed to block the ball so it didn't roll away, but it wasn't a real catch. I made a good throw to second base that kept the runner on first. I knew I needed two things; more practice before a game and my own glove. Getting some practice was easy. My new friend Denny and I agreed to pitch, swing, and catch after school every day. But getting a glove wasn't going to be so easy.

Denny had a new glove. "I oiled the leather to make it softer and easier to grab the ball," he said. "See how it has a preformed pocket to help you catch it?"

I tried it on my hand and then I pounded a baseball into its pocket just like I had seen other guys do. "Yeah, I sure wish I had a new glove," I said, "just like this one."

I thought about baseball most of the time, and so did the rest of the guys. We talked about the Red Sox and the Yankees; we memorized batting averages and compared the records of Babe Ruth, Lou Gehrig, and Jackie Robinson. The great players were my heroes. I knew I'd never play like them, but I wanted to play well, and a new glove would definitely make me a better player.

I could have asked my mom and dad for the money, but I knew they didn't have enough for things like baseball gloves. I did get a weekly allowance, but only 21 cents a week. I figured it would take me a long, long time to save enough for a baseball glove.

On my way home from Denny's I always walked by the Harco Sporting Goods store. I didn't go in there much because the things I wanted always cost a lot more than I had. Then one day as I passed the store, a man walked out and an open door let the smell of leather drift past my nose. That smell just grabbed me and pulled me inside.

"Can I help you, son?" asked the store clerk.

"No," I said, "I just want to look at the baseball gloves."

The gloves came in a variety of colors, from golden tan to reddish-brown to black. Most of them cost between $7 and $10, but the one that got my attention was only $5.95.

"How come this glove is longer than the others?" I asked the clerk.

"That's because it's for the first baseman," he replied. "At first base you have to reach for the throw and still keep your foot on the bag."

"Who's Johnny Mize?" I asked, pointing to the signature burned into the leather.

"He's the first baseman for the New York Giants, and a good player, too."

I slipped my left hand into the glove and threw a baseball into its pocket with my right. It felt so good. Then I put my nose in the pocket and inhaled the strong scent of leather. OOOOOO! This would make me a terrific player, I thought.

I thanked the clerk and left dreaming about catching the ball and tagging a runner out at first base. By the time I got home I had decided to tell my mom and dad about the glove. My dad didn't say anything, but I could tell he was thinking about it.

The next morning at breakfast, Dad said to me, "Your mother and I have talked it over, and we can give you five dollars for a baseball glove. That's a lot of money for us, and it's the best we can do."

"But the glove costs $5.95," I whined.

"Well, I don't know what else to tell you. If you want that glove you'll just have to find another way to get it," he said.

I was so disappointed that I almost forgot to say, "Thank you."

At school, my mind was not on my work, and as I stared out the window Mrs. Averill said, "David, are you with us today?" No, I wasn't there. I just didn't know what to do. I had more money in my pocket than I ever had before, but it wasn't enough for the baseball glove that would make me a better player. If I didn't spend any of my allowance for the next four weeks I could save another dollar, but in four weeks school vacation almost would be here. I needed a glove NOW!

After school I went downtown to Harco Sporting Goods and looked at the glove again. I told the clerk I wanted the glove but that I had only five dollars. "Gee, I'm sorry, kid. I'd like to help you out, but I can't change the price. Why don't you see what they have in Woolworth's?"

Who would go to Woolworth's to buy a REAL baseball glove? I wondered. But, I didn't know what else to do, so I went down the street to Woolworth's.

Baseballs, softballs, and bats were in the toy section. There were some gloves, but none that looked like the ones at Harco. Then I saw a combo package of a baseball in a baseball mitt and a baseball bat to go with them for only $4.95! I had $5.00 that would pay for them all.

The bat and the ball looked just like the ones that I was used to, but the glove was a sickly yellow color, and it didn't have all the fingers held together with the leather thong. There was not much of a "pocket," either. The other gloves that were on display looked about the same but didn't come with a ball and bat. This glove was NOT what I had dreamed of. Should I buy a glove just to have something now, or wait? No one could help me with the decision, so I bought the combo package and took it home.

"Well, what a good shopper you are," announced my Mom when she saw what I bought. She said she was proud of me. But I wasn't proud of me and I wasn't happy about the glove.

I used it when I had to, but I was ashamed of it and of myself for wasting my money on a glove I didn't really like. I never asked for another glove, and by the time I earned enough money from a paper route to buy a better one, the other kids my age were playing way beyond my ability, and my passion for baseball had become limited to watching the Sox or the Giants play the game.

Sample Mentor Texts

Sample 1

"Ready?"

"Ready."

"Now?"

"Soon."

"Look, look; see for yourself! Do the scientists really know? Will it happen today, will it?"

The children pressed to each other like so many roses, so many weeds, intermixed, peering out for a look at the hidden sun.

It rained.

It had been raining for seven years; thousands upon thousands of days compounded and filled from one end to the other with rain, with the drum and gush of water, with the sweet crystal fall of showers and the concussion of storms so heavy they were tidal waves come over the islands.

— from "All Summer in a Day" by Ray Bradbury

Sample 2

What they don't understand about birthdays and what they never tell you is that when you're eleven, you're also ten, and nine, and eight, and seven, and six, and five, and four, and three, and two, and one. And when you wake up on your eleventh birthday you expect to feel eleven, but you don't. You open your eyes and everything's just like yesterday, only it's today. And you don't feel eleven at all. You feel like you're still ten. And you are—underneath the year that makes you eleven.

— from "Eleven" by Sandra Cisneros

Sample 3

None of them knew the color of the sky. Their eyes glanced level, and were fastened upon the waves that swept toward them. These waves were of the hue of slate, save for the tops, which were of foaming white, and all of the men knew the colors of the sea. The horizon narrowed and widened, and dipped and rose, and at all times its edge was jagged with waves that seemed thrust up in points like rocks.

Many a man ought to have a bathtub larger than the boat which here rode upon the sea. These waves were most wrongfully and barbarously abrupt and tall, and each froth-top was a problem in small-boat navigation.

—from "The Open Boat" by Stephen Crane

Sample 4

Even my own cousin Ben was there—riding away, in the ringing of bicycle bells down the road. Every time I came to watch them—them riding round and round enjoying themselves—they scooted off like crazy on their bikes.

They can't keep doing that. They'll see!

I only want to be with Nat, Aldo, Jimmy, and Ben. It's no fair reason they don't want to be with me. Anybody could go off their head for that. Anybody! A girl can not, not, let boys get away with it all the time.
— from "Becky and the Wheels-and-Brake Boys" by James Berry

Sample 5

Once on a time when wishes were aplenty, a fisherman and his wife lived by the side of the sea. All that they ate came out of the sea. Their hut was covered with the finest mosses that kept them cool in the summer and warm in the winter. And there was nothing they needed or wanted except a child.

Each morning, when the moon touched down behind the water and the sun rose up behind the plains, the wife would say to the fisherman, "You have your boat and your nets and your lines. But I have no baby to hold in my arms." And again, in the evening, it was the same. She would weep and wail and rock the cradle that stood by the hearth. But year in and year out the cradle stayed empty.
— from "Greyling" by Jane Yolen

Sample 6

One dollar and eighty-seven cents. That was all. And sixty cents of it was in pennies. Pennies saved one and two at a time by bulldozing the grocer and the vegetable man and the butcher until one's cheeks burned with silent imputation of parsimony that such close dealing implied. Three times Della counted it. One dollar and eighty-seven cents. And the next day would be Christmas.

There was clearly nothing to do but flop down on the shabby little couch and howl. So Della did it. Which instigates the moral reflection that life is made up of sobs, sniffles, and smiles, with sniffles predominating.
—from "The Gift of the Magi" by O. Henry

Sample 7

Marley was dead, to begin with. There was no doubt whatever about that. The register of his burial was signed by the clergyman, the clerk, the undertaker, and the chief mourner. Scrooge signed it. And Scrooge's name was good upon 'Change for anything he chose to put his hand to.
—from "A Christmas Carol" by Charles Dickens

Writing Circle Peer Response to a Short Story

Student writer: _____ Story title: _____

Peer responder: _____ Date: _____

Student writer's request to responder: Ask a question about something you would like to learn from your responder: _____

_____

Peer responder:

1. Reply to the student writer's request as written above.

_____

_____

2. Write a sentence or two describing the setting or vivid action from the story that was particularly memorable because of the writer's language.

_____

_____

3. Locate at least two examples of characterization in the story and write a phrase from each example next to the type of characterization.

   a. Direct description: _____

   b. What the character says: _____

   c. What the character does: _____

   d. What others say about the character: _____

   e. How others react to the character: _____

4. Write a sentence from the story that summarizes the major conflict:

_____

_____

5. Summarize the plot of the story in one sentence, filling in these blanks:

   In the beginning, _____,

   but then in the middle _____,

   and finally, in the end, _____.

6. What does the story reveal about human nature? _____

_____

PART IV:
Guide to Assessment and Evaluation

Ask students about grading and they are likely to say that in the best of all possible classrooms, in the best of all possible worlds, grades don't matter. And we might even agree, except we know it's human nature for us to want to know how we're doing, whether we're learning to shoot baskets, solve an equation, bake a cake, run a marathon, or write a composition. We need to know the extent to which we are succeeding and where we need more practice or instruction. That kind of assessment is necessary for growth in learning to do anything from hitting a tennis ball to playing the piano to writing for real audiences.

And periodically, as we practice our learning, we want to know how we measure up to a standard or model of performance—in short, the results of our efforts need to be *evaluated*, i.e., graded, so that we know what we have accomplished, and we also know where we must direct additional efforts.

Assessment and Evaluation Are Two Related but Distinct Processes

Before we go any further, we should acknowledge that, like many terms in education, different people use the related terms *assessment* and *evaluation* in somewhat different ways. We want you to know how we are using these terms.

What Assessment Is All About

We define *assessment* as a formative, ongoing process that teachers use to inform instructional decisions, reflect specific outcomes, and provide feedback to students. The goal is to help both teachers and students appreciate students' growth as language users and to determine what students still need to learn. At its core, effective assessment is a matter of day-to-day, informal information gathering and keen observation of regular learning situations, such as practice activities and classroom participation.

Grades are no more appropriate for these kinds of learning activities than for basketball clinic practice, warm-up exercises, or drop-shot tryouts. These routines are necessary pregame activities so that, when the real game begins, the athletes can play well and have a good chance of winning. During all the practice work the coach is, in fact, engaged in assessment—observing the players' strength, their skills development, and their readiness for the game.

We, the English language arts teachers, are the language coaches, constantly assessing our students' skills development and language strengths to determine the extent of their growth as competent readers, writers, and speakers. Assessment for us, as for the basketball coach, is the process of determining the extent to which our students have mastered the concepts and competencies of the game. For the language arts coach, that means the extent to which students can:

- Understand the writing and revising process in a variety of modes and purposes
- Use the English language to write clearly, coherently, and purposefully for a variety of audiences
- Apply their understanding of English language structure to read mature, grade-appropriate texts for meaning and even insight

For example, if a student is having problems recognizing relevant, specific details to develop a topic, then we have to respond with more direct teaching and guided practice to help him or her learn what he or she needs to know and be able to select details that are relevant to the topic and to incorporate them into the composition as a competent language user. What these emerging writers do not need is a grade for their learning efforts. But there is a right time for grading, and we discuss that next.

What Evaluation Is All About

We define *evaluation* as a summative process aimed at assigning a value to what students have learned. What they have learned is demonstrated by a particular product that reflects their application and understanding of skills. Another way of stating this is that the product reflects the extent to which students have mastered what they have practiced. This product is given a grade—a grade determined by criteria for mastery that have been clear to students from the beginning of the learning and all during the weeks and months of practice.

The products take many formats, but for our purposes these demonstrations are poems, stories, essays, reviews, letters, and news stories. These authentic compositions are the real thing, just as basketball games and other sports events are the real thing for athletes. Unlike practice sessions, games are played for scores; the same is true for students' language products.

The Role of Rubrics

Creating rubrics may seem difficult initially, but teachers who use them regularly (and this includes both of us) recognize that the very process of creating them helps teachers focus on what their students need to know and be able to do. The rubrics also help students understand what they need to learn and be able to do. We believe in involving students themselves in the evaluation process of their mastery products. Thus for each of the steps below we include students as much as possible in the creation of the rubrics.

In this section, we walk you through the process of creating a particular rubric, Rubric One, and then provide an example of this rubric (page 124). Next, you'll find two alternative formats for rubrics, with brief commentary.

Determining the Task to Be Evaluated

We find task-specific rubrics to be useful for the very reason that they are so focused on a particular, identified product. Once you determine that your students are far enough along in their learning about a particular writing assignment and in their application of revision strategies to be evaluated, you can choose a task for this evaluation. Involve students in the timing of the evaluation. For example, if they have completed a good deal of work on writing free-verse poems, you and they together might come up with a task that requires them to create a collection (five or six, perhaps) of poems. From the moment the task is assigned, students are aware that their product will ultimately be evaluated via a task-specific rubric. In fact, the next step is to determine with them the nature of that rubric.

Determining and Defining the Qualities to Be Evaluated

Based on what students have learned from their practice work on, for example, writing free-verse poems, we now need to decide, with them, what qualities are important enough to be included in the rubric. Considering the context, they are likely to volunteer "form" and "language use" and "imagery." You can nudge students along, if necessary, and suggest these additional categories: "content" (sometimes called "meaning"), "development," and "organization." Help them streamline ahead of time and suggest that, for the purposes of the rubric, "form" can be folded within "content." It's worth noting that there are no hard-and-fast rules. You'll need to adapt each rubric somewhat to address the specific task and situation. For example, we've found that it's sometimes appropriate to include "development" and "organization" within the "content" category as well, but for this example, we have retained them as separate qualities.

The next step is to help students define what each of these qualities really means and how the meaning can be stated clearly enough to lend itself to evaluation. Allow sufficient time for you and your students to create definitions that are appropriate for the task and understood by everyone. Don't be afraid to use the vocabulary of evaluation; give your students the opportunity to become familiar with the language teachers use to evaluate students' work.

A sample set of definitions for these qualities follows:

- **Content**: The extent to which the response is appropriate to the task
- **Development**: The extent to which ideas and images are specific and relevant to the subject of the task
- **Organization**: The extent to which the response exhibits direction, shape, and coherence
- **Language Use**: The extent to which the response reveals an awareness of purpose and effective use of words (if you decide to highlight fluency and/or imagery as instructional goals to be graded, this would be the place to do so)
- **Conventions**: The extent to which the response is grammatically correct

Determining and Defining the Levels of Response

Once you have decided on the qualities appropriate for the task assigned, you need to decide on the levels of response for your rubric. We often use a four-level rubric, 3 being the top (A, or Excellent), 2 the middle (B, or Good), 1 the low (C, or Adequate), and 0 indicating an incoherent or irrelevant response. We generally don't give a letter grade below C on these writing and revising activities; rather, we give the student some teaching support and another opportunity to complete the assignment. Some teachers prefer a five-level rubric, 4 being A, 3 being B, 2 being C, and 1 acknowledging the student's effort to fulfill the assignment. The 0 still indicates an incoherent or irrelevant response.

Your next task is to define those levels of response in clear, descriptive language. Avoid evaluative terms such as "good," "excellent," or "poor" in your descriptions. Instead, describe the student's performance for each category.

Rubric One

You can use this kind of rubric to grade your students' pieces holistically. You can also circle those descriptions on each rubric that reflect a student's work. That way the student can see what he or she has done well and where he or she needs to improve. In other words, the holistic grade is explained.

It's important to realize that a holistic score is not determined by adding the number of 3's, 2's, and 1's and then dividing them by 5 (or however many qualities you identify for evaluation). That procedure can result in a skewed grade, one not reflective of the extent to which the student has demonstrated her or his understanding of the task and the skills being measured. In fact, you may weigh some qualities more than others. For example, with a story or essay response, "content" and "development" might be given more weight than "grammar." With a poem, "language use" and "organization" might be more heavily weighted. Then again, you may decide to give equal weight to all qualities.

It all depends on what you have emphasized in your teaching and in the assignment. So here's where your good teacher judgment comes into play. By circling the most accurate description of responses to the evaluation qualities, you indicate to students their strengths and weaknesses, but then you make an overall (i.e., holistic) judgment of their performance. A sample of this rubric is shown on page 124.

Rubric Two

An example of another rubric format you may prefer is given on page 125. Rubric Two works well particularly with free-verse poetry and the letter to an author. This kind of more loosely structured rubric eliminates numbers (unless you choose to incorporate them) and encourages holistic evaluation in broad strokes like Excellent, Good, and Adequate. The students whose work isn't "adequate" should be encouraged to try again with help, of course, to achieve at least an adequate overall grade.

If you wish, you can assign a percentage to each quality on this rubric, weighting certain qualities as appropriate for the assignment, and determine the final grade arithmetically. However, we encourage the holistic approach.

A few words about the final two items on this rubric. The Commendations block is the place to include your positive comments about the student's work—what you especially liked in the piece, what the student is doing well, or how he or she is showing improvement. The Recommendations block is a dedicated space for you to offer suggestions about how the student can improve his or her response. Of course, the understanding is that revisions are encouraged! The commendations and recommendations you offer should help all students build on their achievements and be guided toward success in their revisions.

Rubric Three

Rubric Three (page 126) works well for products such as the letter to an author and the short short story. Like Rubric Two, this one lends itself to holistic scoring. Note that the descriptions we provide in this model are general; you will probably want to make them more task-specific. Just be sure to describe performance levels objectively. The numbers listed in the left-hand column are the evaluative levels, which you can circle and also label with evaluative language if you wish—Excellent, Good, Adequate, or Incomplete.

Regardless of the products you choose for your evaluations or the rubrics you create to measure your students' learning, make sure you have given them plenty of guided practice and that they understand the criteria by which their mastery work will be graded. In this way, grading becomes part of the learning process and an effective way for you to communicate to your students and their parents the extent of each student's learning.

Closing Thoughts

We sincerely hope this book has helped you in your efforts to promote authentic, real writing and revising in your students' lives. May you continue to nurture young readers, writers, and thinkers by empowering them with knowledge and strategies for using our dynamic language. We salute the bold, brave, committed teachers who convey the power of language to their students by teaching them writing and revising with meaningful classroom practices that incorporate humor as well as academic rigor. As a result, many young speakers and writers will communicate, enlighten, and inspire their audiences with elegance and eloquence—and they will be able to do so for life.

Rubric One

Name of student: _____ Overall grade: _____

	3 Responses at this level	2 Responses at this level	1 Responses at this level	0 Responses at this level
Content: the extent to which the response is appropriate to the task	Fulfills all the requirements of the task; reflects clear thematic idea	Fulfills most of the requirements of the task; thematic idea not always clear	Fulfills few of the requirements of the task	The response is irrelevant or incoherent
Development: the extent to which ideas and images are specific and relevant to the subject of the task	The images are relevant, clear, and appropriate to the thematic idea	Most of the images are clear and appropriate to the topic; some relevance to the thematic idea	Few images, with little relevance to the thematic idea	The response is irrelevant or incoherent
Organization: the extent to which the response exhibits direction, shape, and coherence	Establishes and maintains a clear focus; follows a logical sequence of ideas	Is generally focused, but some irrelevant details; shows a clear attempt at organization	Does not establish and maintain a focus; shows little or no organization	The response is irrelevant or incoherent
Language Use: the extent to which the response reveals an awareness of purpose and effective use of words	Is fluent and easy to read; uses vivid and appropriate language	Is easy to read; uses appropriate language	Is readable; uses some appropriate language	The response is irrelevant or incoherent
Grammar: the extent to which the response is grammatically correct	The piece is grammatically correct for the task	The piece is generally correct for the task	The piece is minimally correct for the task; there are errors in parts of speech and/or parts of the sentence	The piece demonstrates a lack of understanding of the parts of speech and the parts of the sentence

Rubric Two

Name of student: _____   Overall grade: _____

Qualities to Be Evaluated	Excellent	Good
Adequate		
Content		
Focus on subject		
Clarity (and appropriateness of images)		
Knowledge of the subject		
Development		
Fully developed idea		
Specific, relevant details		
Organization		
Logical flow from beginning to end		
Coherence		
Language		
Appropriate and effective use of word choice		
Tone		

Commendations:

Recommendations:

Rubric Three

Name of student: _____ Overall grade: _____

4   Complete fulfillment of the task:

Consistently uses correct and varied sentence structures

Relevant and engaging details

Logical development

Sophisticated use of language

Consistently correct language mechanics

3   Fulfillment of the task:

Generally correct sentence structures

Relevant details

Correct use of language

Few errors in mechanics; those that do appear do not interfere with meaning

2   Some effort to fulfill the task:

Some correct sentence structures, but inconsistent

Few details, some irrelevant

Generally correct use of language

Some errors in mechanics that may interfere with meaning

1   Failure to complete the task:

Few correct sentence structures

Few details

Inaccurate use of language

Errors in language mechanics that interfere with meaning

Revision Lessons You'll Love to Teach © 2008 by Ruth Townsend Story and Cathleen F. Greenwood, Scholastic Professional.

Bibliography

Akeret, R. U. (2000). *Photolanguage: How photos reveal the fascinating stories of our lives and relationships.* New York: W. W. Norton.

Angelillo, J. (2005). *Making revision matter.* New York: Scholastic.

Blasingame, J., & Bushman, J. H. (2004). *Teaching writing in middle and secondary schools.* Upper Saddle River, NJ: Pearson Prentice Hall.

Bomer, R. (1995). *Time for meaning: Crafting literate lives in middle and high school.* Portsmouth, NH: Heinemann.

Bourke-White, M., & Callahan, S. (1972). *The photographs of Margaret Bourke-White.* New York: New York Graphic Society.

Ciccone, E. (2001). A place for talk in writer's workshop. *The Quarterly, 23* (4).

Coles, R. (1990). *The call of stories.* Boston: Houghton Mifflin.

Elbow, P. (1998). *Writing with power.* New York: Oxford University Press.

Fletcher, R., & Portalupi, J. (1998). *Craft lessons: Teaching writing K–8.* Portland, ME: Stenhouse.

Gilmore, B. (2007). *"Is it done yet?": Teaching adolescents the art of revision.* Portsmouth, NH: Heinemann.

Grambs, D. (1995). *The describer's dictionary.* New York: W. W. Norton.

Graves, D. (1994). *A fresh look at writing.* Portsmouth, NH: Heinemann.

Heard, G. (2002). *The revision toolbox: Teaching techniques that work.* Portsmouth, NH: Heinemann.

Killgallon, D., & Killgallon, J. (2000). *Sentence composing for elementary school.* Portsmouth, NH: Heinemann.

Lane, B. (1993). *After the end: Teaching and learning creative revision.* Portsmouth, NH: Heinemann.

Lange, D. (2003). *Dorothea Lange: Photographs of a lifetime.* New York: Aperture.

McCurry, S. (1999). *Portraits.* New York: Phaidon.

Murray, D. (1984). *Write to learn.* Ft. Worth, TX: Holt, Rinehart and Winston.

Murray, D. (1994). *The craft of revision* (2nd ed.) Ft. Worth, TX: Holt, Rinehart and Winston.

Robb, L. (2004). *Nonfiction writing from the inside out.* New York: Scholastic.

Romano, T. (2004). *Crafting authentic voice.* Portsmouth, NH: Heinemann.

Sizoo, B. (2001). *Teaching powerful writing.* New York: Scholastic.

Smolan, R., & Cohen, D. (1986). *A day in the life of America.* New York: HarperCollins.

Stanek, L. W. (1996). *Writing your life: Putting your past on paper.* NY: HarperCollins.

Steichen, E. (2002). *The family of man.* New York: Museum of Modern Art.

Story, R. T., & Greenwood, C. F. (2005). *Grammar lessons you'll love to teach.* New York: Scholastic.

Zinsser, W. (2006). *On writing well.* (30th anniversary ed.) New York: HarperCollins.

Literature Cited

Beltz, Justin, Ed. *The Best Teen Writing of 2007: Selections From the Scholastic Art and Writing Awards.* NY: Alliance for Young Artists and Writers, 2007.

Berry, James. "Becky and the Wheels-and-Brake Boys" in *A Thief in the Village and Other Stories of Jamaica*, pp. 1–11. NY: Penguin, 1990.

Bloor, Edward. *Tangerine.* Orlando, FL: Harcourt, 2006.

Bradbury, Ray. "All Summer in a Day" in *Impact: Fifty short short stories*, pp. 91–97. Fannie Safier, ed. NY: Harcourt, 1986.

Bronte, Charlotte. *Jane Eyre.* NY: Penguin, 2006.

Brown, Dan. *The Da Vinci Code.* NY: Anchor, 2006.

Christie, Agatha. *And Then There Were None.* NY: St. Martin's, 2004.

Cisneros, Sandra. "Eleven" in *Vintage Cisneros*, pp. 40–45. NY: Random House, 2004.

Crane, Stephen. "The Open Boat" in *Great Short Works of Stephen Crane*, pp. 277–292. NY: HarperCollins, 2004.

Curtis, Christopher Paul. *The Watsons Go to Birmingham—1963.* NY: Bantam, 1995.

Dickens, Charles. *A Christmas Carol.* NY: Simon and Schuster, 1967.

Dickens, Charles. *Oliver Twist.* NY: Penguin, 2002.

Durrell, Gerald and Lee. *Durrell in Russia.* NY: Simon and Schuster, 1988.

Fitzgerald, F. Scott. *The Great Gatsby.* NY: Scribner, 1999.

Haddix, Margaret Peterson. *Among the Betrayed.* NY: Aladdin, 2002.

Haddon, Mark. *The Curious Incident of the Dog at Nighttime.* NY: Doubleday, 2003.

Henry, O. *The Gift of the Magi.* New York: Simon & Schuster, 2006.

Hudson, W. H. *Green Mansions.* Charleston, SC: Bibliobazaar, 2007.

Huxley, Aldous. *Brave New World.* NY: HarperCollins, 1991.

Jackson, Shirley. "The Lottery" in *Points of View: An Anthology of Short Stories*, pp. 556–565. James Moffett and Kenneth R. McElheny, eds. NY: New American Library, 1995.

Kingsolver, Barbara. *The Bean Trees.* NY: HarperCollins, 1988.

London, Jack. *White Fang.* NY: Scholastic, 2001.

Rash, Ron. *Saints at the River.* NY: Picador, 2004.

Still, James. *River of Earth.* Lexington, KY: University Press of Kentucky, 1978.

Whitman, Walt. "Song of Myself" in *Leaves of Grass.* NY: Heritage Press, 1855. Copyright 1855 by Doubleday, Doran and company, Inc. and reprinted by special permission. pp. 25–82.

Whitman, Walt. "Great Are the Myths" in *Leaves of Grass.* NY: Heritage Press, 1855. Copyright 1855 by Doubleday, Doran and company, Inc. and reprinted by special permission. pp. 489–490.

Yolen, Jane. *Greyling.* NY: Philomel, 1991.